Dearest Kiersten,
    Some fun reading
for you down time
while in the hospital!
        with love, Jen O.
                    xoxo

Popular Mechanics

THE
POCKET GENIUS

563 FACTS THAT MAKE YOU THE SMARTEST PERSON IN THE ROOM

HEARST BOOKS
New York

HEARST BOOKS
New York

An Imprint of Sterling Publishing
387 Park Avenue South
New York, NY 10016

Book Design by Jon Chaiet

Library of Congress Cataloging-in-Publication Data
Popular mechanics, the pocket genius : 563 facts that make you the smartest person in the room.
  p. cm.
ISBN 978-1-58816-879-5
1. Questions and answers. 2. Intellect—Problems, exercises, etc. I. Popular mechanics (Chicago, Ill. : 1959)
AG195.P66 2012
031.02--dc23
                           2011035076
10 9 8 7 6 5 4 3 2 1

Popular Mechanics is a registered trademark of Hearst Communications, Inc.
www.popularmechanics.com

For information about custom editions, special sales, premium and corporate purchases, please contact Sterling Special Sales Department at 800-805-5489 or specialsales@sterlingpublishing.com.

Distributed in Canada by Sterling Publishing
c/o Canadian Manda Group, 165 Dufferin Street
Toronto, Ontario, Canada M6K 3H6
Distributed in the United Kingdom by GMC Distribution Services
Castle Place, 166 High Street, Lewes, East Sussex, England BN7 1XU
Distributed in Australia by Capricorn Link (Australia) Pty. Ltd.
P.O. Box 704, Windsor, NSW 2756 Australia

Manufactured in China
ISBN 978-1-58816-879-5

TABLE OF CONTENTS

TABLE OF CONTENTS

CHAPTER 1

SCIENCE & TECHNOLOGY

So maybe your DIY life doesn't involve robots, teleportation, or DNA manipulation. These are, however, big ideas that massively changed the way we live. Let's see what you know about them.

INNOVATIONS AND INVENTIONS

If it doesn't come from nature, then it was once an invention. But how much do you know about the once brilliant—and the still brilliant—things that were born of human ingenuity?

1. TRUE OR FALSE?

We've all used Google maps to check out the street we grew up on, but viewers using Google's satellite photos and aerial imagery have also been able to find images of the Playboy Mansion, a rendering of Oprah Winfrey plowed into an Arizona field, and nuclear test sites online.

2. Drivers in the Chinese city of Leiyang are using a bridge built primarily of what material?

A PVC pipes
B Bamboo
C Glass
D Wire

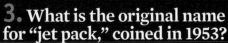

3. What is the original name for "jet pack," coined in 1953?

4. The Arthur Ravenel Jr. Bridge in Charleston, South Carolina, is 3.5 miles long. No, we're not going to ask you who Arthur Ravenel, Jr. was. We just want to know if the bridge used more bolts or more cubic yards of concrete in its construction.

5. No, it isn't a race to the sun (talk about a hot foot). What does the annual Solar Decathlon, sponsored by the Department of Energy, challenge students to do?

Ⓐ Design solar-powered homes
Ⓑ Design solar-powered cars
Ⓒ Design solar-powered appliances
Ⓓ Race in a marathon to raise awareness of renewables

6. The tin can was invented in 1810. But how many years did we have to wait for the twist can opener to be invented?

A 3—or the number of minutes it took six people to bob for 361 apples to set the world record in 2010

B 28—or the number of letters in the Esperanto alphabet

C 36—or the number of UK gallons in a standard beer barrel

D 48—or the number of pounds that a trout caught in 2009 weighed (it would have been the world record if it weren't a genetically modified fish that escaped from a fish farm)

7. Biomechatronics combines biology, mechanics, and electronics to create what?

A Artificial intelligence

B Interactive computer games

C Prosthetics

D Cyborgs

8. In 1964, Robert Moog's breakthrough electronic synthesizer was controlled by a keyboard. What controlled earlier synthesizers?

9. In 1955, Patent No. 2,717,437 was issued to George de Mestral for a fabric inspired by burrs that stuck to his dog's fur. What did he invent?

10.

An estimated 90 percent of plate glass is produced by floating molten glass on a bath of what?

Ⓐ Salt water
Ⓑ Molten tin
Ⓒ Warm milk
Ⓓ Melted steel

11. An early version of Astroturf, named Chemgrass, was used as far back as 1964.

12. Each of the animals below have had a prosthesis to replace a damaged limb. Can you match the material used in the prostheses to the correct animal?

A Thai elephant's leg	**Titanium**
A Japanese dolphin's tail	**Fiberglass & silicone**
An American eagle's beak	**Rubber**

13. Researchers have constructed a simple modular robot that can assemble exact copies of itself. Why would NASA be interested in these robots?

16. Which side won the first-ever human versus robot arm-wrestling match?

14. What does the term "Uncanny Valley," coined in 1970, refer to?

A The repulsion felt by test subjects when presented with robots that appear almost, but not quite, human

B The unexplained grooves in the surface of unexplored planets

C The area in Roswell where wreckage fell from the sky

D Cos/sin waves

15. If a robot is anthropomimetic, what does that mean?

17. Robots used by American troops in Iraq to investigate or handle improvised explosives are sent to the Joint Robotics Repair Facility at Camp Victory in Iraq when they give out. How many robots does the shop handle a year? (Hint: It's also the number of red-winged blackbirds that fell from the Arkansas sky on January 1, 2011.)

19. **TRUE OR FALSE?**
Fast-food restaurants have tested an artificial intelligence system that predicts what customers will order based on the make of car they drive.

18. The number of U.S. nuclear reactors reached its apex in 1990. How many reactors existed at that time?

Ⓐ 28—or the number of singers who performed as part of the boy band Menudo from 1977-1997

Ⓑ 112—or the number of miles biked as part of the Ironman Triathlon

Ⓒ 154—or the number of Shakespearean sonnets

Ⓓ 180—or the maximum possible score after one turn at darts

20. July 13 is "Embrace Your Geekness Day." It's also the birthday of a Hungarian puzzle inventor. Can you guess who it is?

21. What does a mobile infrared transmitter (MIRD) do?

22. Match the invention to the year it was invented.

Gas grill	1960
TV remote control	1955
Smoke detector	1969
Sony Walkman	1979
MRI	1973
Superglue	1958

23. In what year did CD sales peak?

24. What were the first charcoal briquettes made from?

Ⓐ Wood scraps left over from Model T production

Ⓑ Pure coal

Ⓒ A farmer's combination of wheat and wood

Ⓓ Cattle dung

25. Each of the six U.S. Deep-Water Assessment and Reporting systems in the Pacific Ocean combines a surface buoy with a BPR, which detects tsunamis by measuring small changes on the ocean floor. What does BPR stand for?

26. TRUE OR FALSE?

There are 43 quintillion possible configurations of a Rubik's Cube.

28.
Thanks to the polymer poly-HEMA hydrogel, we now have what now-common disposable innovation?

29.
Where did the first ATM open in 1969?

ⓐ Los Angeles, California
ⓑ Rockville Centre, New York
ⓒ Las Vegas, Nevada
ⓓ Los Alamos, New Mexico

27.

The highest bridge in the world (in southern France) is 62 feet taller than the Eiffel Tower which is 1,125 feet high.

How long would it take a bottle of Bordeaux to hit the ground if you dropped it from the deck of the bridge?

ⓐ 7.4 seconds
ⓑ 26.4 seconds
ⓒ 1 minute
ⓓ 90 seconds

COMPUTERS, TELEVISIONS, AND OTHER ELECTRONICS

It seems that every six months, something innovative happens in the world of computers and television technology. Let's see how much you know about past innovations in this area.

30. What do you call a computer-savvy person who uses DIY skills to customize his PC, often transforming it into a practical work of art?

31. TRUE OR FALSE?
Dragging your unwanted computer programs into the trash will free up room on your hard drive.

32. What does URL stand for?

33. What does HTML stand for?

36. Which is the best way to save electricity: turn off your PC or set it to "sleep"?

34. The term Wi-Fi, which originated in the late 1990s, is a pun on hi-fi. What does Wi-Fi stand for?

35. Your computer has its fair share of spinning, whirring, and vibrating parts. There are many things you can do to reduce the noise they generate, but which of the following won't help?

Ⓐ Replace small fans with larger, quieter ones
Ⓑ Buffer the hard-drive-holding screws with rubber washers
Ⓒ Reboot regularly
Ⓓ Apply peel-and-stick barrier panels

37. Most new WiFi routers now have MIMO technology. What does MIMO stand for?

....

38. TRUE OR FALSE?
Computer power supplies convert household AC electricity to DC.

39. FILL IN THE BLANK:
computers use a _____, or base-two mathematical systems.

41. TRUE OR FALSE?
It is possible for the ink in printer cartridges to evaporate.

40. The Antikythera Mechanism, an ancient analog computer discovered in fragments by a diver off the coast of Greece, was used to do what?

42. What is RSS (the technology that uses the XML format to bring headlines from newspapers and blogs directly to you) abbreviated from?

45. TRUE OR FALSE?
Spyware and viruses have the same purpose and the same vectors of infection.

43. IBM built the RAMAC in 1956. What was it?

44.
Early computers were limited in speed in part because vacuum tubes could only switch on and off approximately 10,000 times per second. Transistors, however, can do the same thing more than how many times per second?

Ⓐ **Thirty million**
Ⓑ **Three hundred million**
Ⓒ **Three billion**
Ⓓ **Three hundred billion**

46. TRUE OR FALSE?

Reformatting your hard drive is the best way to get rid of information on your computer before you ditch it.

48.

A DDoS is a brute-force attack that uses hijacked computers to overwhelm a target network with bogus requests and data. What does DDoS stand for?

47.

How much did ENIAC, the first general-purpose computer, weigh?

A Nearly **3,000 pounds**— equal to the combined weight of seventeen average American men

B Nearly **30,000 pounds**—the size of a large whale shark

C Nearly **3 tons**—or equal to three 1967 Volkswagen Beetles

D Nearly **30 tons**—or equal to five large Asian bull elephants

49. The Roadrunner supercomputer was the first computer to operate at a speed of 1 petaflop, performing a quadrillion calculations per second—twice the speed of the previous record holder. What was its main job?

A To calculate rocket speeds needed to reach outer planets
B To measure heat generated by the sun
C To simulate nuclear weapons tests
D To operate California's electrical grid

50. Modern CRT displays are no longer susceptible from burn-in because of a layer of aluminum behind the phosphor. What is burn-in?

51. TRUE OR FALSE?
The first computer mouse was made primarily of wood.

52. TRUE OR FALSE?
You can back-up your Xbox 360 or Playstation 3 data with a USB drive.

53. TRUE OR FALSE?

Wi-Fi can be blocked or weakened by metal frames, brick, drywall, and anything with water in it.

54. In order to install a graphics card, you need to...

Ⓐ Change your startup settings
Ⓑ Turn off your computer
Ⓒ Unplug your computer
Ⓓ Turn off and unplug your computer

55. Before the operating system loads on your computer, software on the motherboard known as the BIOS governs the configuration of the PC's hardware. What does BIOS stand for?

56. In what year did the Commodore PET, the Apple II, and the Tandy Radio Shack TRS-80 computers all launch?

57. TRUE OR FALSE?

The Z machine, a partially submerged particle accelerator built to generate data for super-computers that simulate nuclear explosions, has produced a temperature of 2 billion degrees Kelvin, hotter than the interior of the sun.

59.

Which uses less power: playing movies from your laptop's hard drive, or playing them from DVDs?

60. Do LCD screens suffer from burn-in?

58. You decided to take your electronic reader to the beach and dropped it in the sand. Which two options won't help you dislodge the particles of sand?

A Push all the buttons.

B Shake the e-reader gently.

C Use canned air.

D Plugging in headphones.

61. What is the name of the type of computer malware that misleads users into installing a rogue security software program on their PC?

62. Which two of the following names were considered for the World Wide Web by creator Tim Berners-Lee?

Ⓐ Mine of Information (MOI)

Ⓑ World Information Resource Enterprise (WIRE)

Ⓒ Highway of Knowledge (HOK)

Ⓓ The Information Mine (TIM)

63. TV remote controls originally used ultrasound technology. What do remote controls use now?

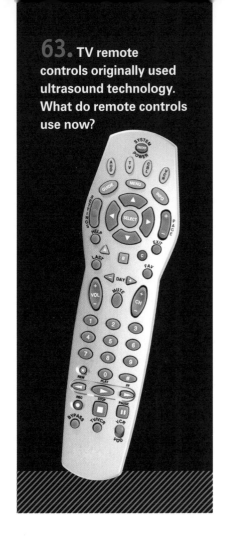

64. You're off to the electronics store to purchase a new TV. You need to evaluate five critical qualities in each television before you plunk down your hard-earned cash. Name three.

66. **TRUE OR FALSE?**
The amount of digital data created by various organizations about you (by financial records, search histories, surveillance shots taken in public places) now exceeds the amount of digital data you actively create (sending e-mails, chatting online, and posting photos).

65. Lithium-ion batteries, found in everything from cell phones to power tools, were the cause of some cases of burning laptops. What was the culprit?

A Damage to the wiring
B Thermal runaway
C Short circuits
D The formation of dendrites

67. Which is worse for your smartphone's battery life: accessing the Internet over Wi-Fi or over the 3G network?

68. TRUE OR FALSE?

If you know it's going to be a long time before you use your lithium-ion battery–powered gadget again, you should run its battery down to just under half of the maximum charge and leave it in the freezer.

70. Many movie theaters use DLP technology. What does DLP stand for?

69. If they remain plugged in, electronic devices still consume power when they're turned off. Match the amount of power each device uses while it's off. (The number in parentheses is the amount of power each device uses while it's on).

Plasma TV (210 watts)	**1.3 watts**
Cable box/digital video recorder (26 watts)	**1 watt**
Nintendo Wii (16 watts)	**26 watts**
DLP projector (296 watts)	**3.6 watts**
Desktop PC (80 watts)	**4.1 watts**
20-volt battery charger (61.8 watts)	**1 watt**

71. Old-time TVs are often referred to as CRTs. What does CRT stand for?

72. Which type of television—plasma or LCD—relies on an electrically charged gas that releases ultraviolet rays?

73. Both plasma TVs and LCD TVs have their advantages and disadvantages. Which of the following are advantages of LCD TVs?

Ⓐ They run at a cooler temperature.
Ⓑ They render deeper, truer blacks.
Ⓒ For the same screen size, they weigh less.
Ⓓ They have a lower contrast ratio.
Ⓔ Static image burn-in is not a problem.

MEDICINE AND THE BODY

This section contains questions about medical matters. But the doctor is out, so you'll have to fend for yourself.

74. What year was the United States declared polio-free?

Ⓐ 1951—the year *An American in Paris* won the Oscar for best picture

Ⓑ 1967—the year *In the Heat of the Night* won the Oscar for best picture

Ⓒ 1979—the year *Kramer vs. Kramer* won the Oscar for best picture

Ⓓ 1984—the year *Amadeus* won the Oscar for best picture

75. Who won the race to sequence the entire human genome—scientist J. Craig Venter and his company or a federally funded project established for that purpose?

76. Defibrillators send electrical currents through the heart. What is the current meant to do?

77. Sudden cardiac arrest occurs when the heart muscle unexpectedly spasms and can no longer pump blood. What causes a heart attack?

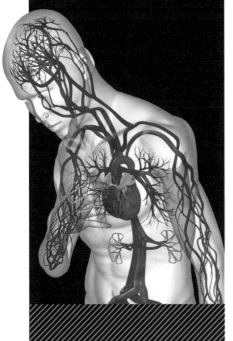

78. What is the longest chain in the human genome?

Ⓐ Chromosome 1
Ⓑ Chromosome 7
Ⓒ Chromosome 15
Ⓓ Chromosome 21

79. TRUE OR FALSE?
A few seconds of exposure to the blue light of an LED will kill the bacteria in your mouth that cause gum disease.

80. What are selective serotonin reuptake inhibitors, or SSRIs, used as?

Ⓐ Antidepressants
Ⓑ Anticoagulants
Ⓒ Antibiotics
Ⓓ All of the above

81. Was the first baby conceived through in vitro fertilization a boy or a girl?

82. TRUE OR FALSE?
As a tool in figuring out how killer flu and other epidemics spread, researchers turn to www.wheresgeorge.com, a website that tracks the movement of dollar bills via user-submitted serial numbers.

83. How many genes does influenza have?

Ⓐ **2**—or the number of weeks it takes for sharks to grow a new set of teeth

Ⓑ **4**—or the number of rocky planets in the solar system (Earth, Mars, Mercury, and Venus)

Ⓒ **8**—or the number of Immortals in Chinese mythology

Ⓓ **16**—or the number of weeks that the Mariah Carey/Boyz II Men song "One Sweet Day" remained at number one on the Billboard charts

84. Which is the most common influenza to affect humans?

A H5N1   **C** H3N2
B H1N1   **D** CBGB

87. Nanosprings, which are found in various human tissues, including hair cells, are actually chains of up to twenty-nine smaller springs of what?

85. Match the approximate percent of oxygen you'll find in each type of air.

Inhaled air	23 percent
Exhaled air	15 to 16 percent
Air at sea level	21 percent

86. Match the medical discovery to the year it was discovered.

The first test-tube baby is born.	1978
The first pacemaker is successfully implanted in a human.	1960
The first coronary bypass surgery is performed.	1967
An MRI machine is used to distinguish healthy tissue from cancer.	1973

88. How many diseases—including Parkinson's and Alzheimer's—are localized to chromosome 1 in the human genome?

Ⓐ 12—the number of pairs of cranial nerves in the average human

Ⓑ 104—the number of Corinthian columns in the Temple of Olympian Zeus, the largest temple ever built in Greece

Ⓒ 356—or, in pounds, slightly more than a professional sumo wrestler's weight (350 pounds)

Ⓓ 660—or the average gestation period for an elephant (in days)

89. Approximately how many genes does a human being have?

90. TRUE OR FALSE?
DNA must be extracted from red blood cells.

91. What does osseointegration allow a prosthetic limb to do?

92. What was the first entire organ to be grown in a lab from a patient's own cells and then implanted into the patient's body? Hint: it happened in 1999.

Ⓐ The liver
Ⓑ The bladder
Ⓒ The kidney
Ⓓ The pancreas

93. You can tell a tree's age by its rings. Scientists can now more accurately determine the year you were born by measuring the amount of radioactive carbon-14 in what?

A Your teeth
B Your bones
C Your hair
D Your internal organs

96. TRUE OR FALSE?
Scientists can re-create an extinct virus.

94. In what year did the United States first use DNA evidence to convict someone?

95. Match the following artificial sweeteners to the factor that each is sweeter than sugar.

Sucralose	30 times sweeter
Aspartame	300 times sweeter
Saccharin	180 times sweeter
Cyclamates	600 times sweeter

97.

Congratulations! You've been named coroner. What branch of forensic science will help you determine how long a bloodstain has been around?

Ⓐ Serology
Ⓑ Hematology
Ⓒ Histology
Ⓓ Oncology

98. Deinococcus radiodurans is listed in *The Guinness Book of World Records* as the "world's toughest bacterium." That's because it can survive exposure to which of the following?

Ⓐ Radiation
Ⓑ Frigid cold
Ⓒ Drought
Ⓒ Acid
Ⓔ All of the above

99. How many unique mutations exist within each person's DNA?

Ⓐ Ten—or the number of official inkblots in the Rorschach inkblot test
Ⓑ Fifteen—or the number of beans in Fifteen Bean Soup
Ⓒ Sixty—or the number of episodes of *The Wire* that were produced over five seasons
Ⓓ More than one hundred—or the number of tiles in a standard Scrabble set

100. How many degrees of freedom exist in the movement and rotation of the lower jaw of a human?

Ⓐ **6**—or the number of strings on a standard guitar
Ⓑ **12**—or the number of basic hues in the color wheel
Ⓒ **18**—or the only number other than zero that equals twice the sum of its digits
Ⓓ **24**—or the number of hours it took Oreo cookies to get 114,619 "likes" on Facebook

101. A gas chromatograph mass spectrometer is one of the most useful tools in forensics. What evidence is it used to detect?

102. Forensic scientists use several tools during a standard autopsy. Which tool in the list below *isn't* used?

Ⓐ **A scalpel**
Ⓑ **A ladle**
Ⓒ **A turkey baster**
Ⓓ **A nail file**

103. The sound of snoring can reach 90 decibels. How loud is that?

Ⓐ **As loud as a plane taking off**
Ⓑ **As loud as a subway train**
Ⓒ **As loud as a sonic boom**
Ⓓ **As loud a stampeding herd of bison**

SCIENCE FUN FACTS

Scientific information doesn't all fit into neat categories. And neither do science trivia questions. Here's some intriguing questions and answers on subjects ranging from teleportation to Higgs boson. What's a Higgs boson? Read on.

104. Which of these three musical groups first used a Moog synthesizer: the Monkees, the Rolling Stones, or the Beatles?

....

105. TRUE OR FALSE?
Gravity is the same everywhere on Earth.

107. Life as we know it needs some kind of...

A Gas
B Liquid
C Solid
D All of the above

106. What shape is a table salt crystal?

108. TRUE OR FALSE?
Researchers have created a "brain" in a dish that can fly an F/A-22 jet simulator.

··

109.
A team of scientists from which two countries has sequenced the Neanderthal genome?

111.
What happened to the first research station in Antarctica?

110.
Match the descriptions of these biological and chemical weapons with their names.

A highly infectious disease caused by touching or breathing in *Bacillus anthracis* spores	Sarin
A toxin produced by the *Clostridium botulinum* bacteria	Pneumonic plague
A historical scourge caused by *Yersinia pestis* bacteria, found in rodents and their fleas	Mustard gas Phosgene
A gas, 2-chloroethane, used during World War I	
A toxic, gaseous agent used in the plastic and pesticide industries	Botulism
An odorless, colorless, tasteless gas that attacks the nervous system	Anthrax

112. At what temperature did construction crews in the Antarctic discover that a crane stops working?

A 32°F—or the average high temperature in January in Ithaca, New York

B −2°F—or Tallahassee, Florida's record-setting low temperature in February 2011

C −20°F—or the average low temperature in Barrow, Alaska

D −40°F—or the only temperature that is the same in Fahrenheit and Celsius

113. Despite what you've seen in *The Fly*, has teleportation of matter ever happened?

114. What is the more popular name of the Higgs boson?

115.

In what year was Dolly the cloned sheep born?

116. TRUE OR FALSE?
Scientists have created a tungsten needle whose point is a single atom wide.

117. With which U.S. president does Charles Darwin share his birthday and birth year every February?

118. Which half-eaten foods are best at preserving traces of DNA evidence? (Choose two of the four below.)

Ⓐ Cheese
Ⓑ Carrots
Ⓒ Chocolate
Ⓓ Bread

119. Name the principle, a cornerstone of modern physics, that states it's impossible to measure something at the subatomic level without altering it.

CHAPTER 2

NATURE

Would you know a bumblebee bat if it bit you? Do you know what type of avalanche is most likely to bury you alive? Or what you should do if you find yourself in a car during a tornado? Check out these intriguing questions about the wild world of nature. The right answers may save your life.

ANIMALS

From dancing birds to glow-in-the-dark piglets, the animal kingdom is filled with strange and wonderful creatures. Even the most ordinary animal can have extraordinary talents. See how much you know about our remarkable feathered, furry, and scaly friends with these brainteasers.

120. Pound for pound, which marsupial has the most ferocious bite on the planet?

121. The Central American manakin bird performs a high-speed dance to attract its mate. To which human dance are its moves similar?

Ⓐ The Moonwalk
Ⓑ The Twist
Ⓒ The Watusi
Ⓓ A circle dance

122. What percent of their time do whales spend at the surface of the ocean?

Ⓐ 3 percent—or the percentage of people who are affected by at least one food allergy

Ⓑ 26 percent—or the percentage of body fat at which an adult male is considered overweight

Ⓒ 48 percent—or the increase in Ford Motor Company's chief executive Alan Mulally's total compensation package in 2011

Ⓓ 98 percent—or the percentage of DNA with largely unknown function, previously known as "junk DNA"

123. How do birds keep their bearings during migration?

Ⓐ Through communication with each other

Ⓑ By staying attuned to sunrise and sunset

Ⓒ By accessing Earth's magnetic field

Ⓓ From evolutionary memory

124. What is bioluminescence?

125. TRUE OR FALSE?
The bumblebee bat, discovered in 1974, was the last new mammal family discovered.

126. Taiwanese scientists injected the DNA from which animal into pig embryos to produce three fluorescent green, glow-in-the-dark piglets?

Ⓐ Glow worm
Ⓑ Jellyfish
Ⓒ Firefly
Ⓓ Squid

128. TRUE OR FALSE?
The first fish that crawled—or slithered—onto dry land were "front-wheel drive," supporting their body weight with their front fins.

127. What percent of deep-ocean animals are bioluminescent?

Ⓐ 10 percent—or the percentage of one's income some Christian denominations believe should be donated to the church through tithing
Ⓑ 35 percent—or the percentage of companies that have a succession plan in place
Ⓒ 55 percent—or the percentage of people fifteen years or older in 2009 who had been married at least once
Ⓓ 90 percent—or the percentage of eggs that women lose by age thirty

129. How many pounds of food can a single swarm of locusts devour in a day?

Ⓐ 2 million—or the weight of the frozen water used annually to create the "Ice!" holiday attraction at Florida's Gaylord Palms Resort and Convention Center near Orlando

Ⓑ 50 million—or how many years ago India began to collide with Asia, forming the Himalayan Mountains

Ⓒ 212 million—or the number of visitors to stores and websites over 2010's Black Friday weekend

Ⓓ 423 million—or the number of miles traveled by the *Phoenix* spacecraft on its trip to Mars

130. You can find the Serrasalmus spilopleura species of fish in the waters of the Pantanal wetlands in Brazil. What kind of fish is this?

132. Which animal's foot is sticky, similar to a Post-it?

131. Match the suburban home invader to its species name.

Bat
Woodchuck
Mouse
Eastern gray squirrel

Peromyscus leucopus
Sciurus carolinensis
Marmota monax
Myotis lucifugus

133.

What is the archerfish known for?

A Its pointed face

B Spitting water at insects on branches more than 2 feet away

C The quickness of its darting tongue, which can extend as much as 18 inches

D Turning different colors based on its environment

134. Which has more resilience: high-resilience rubber, or resilin, the rubberlike protein that allows some insects to float like a bumblebee and jump like a flea?

136. What animal is affected by Colony Collapse Disorder?

135. Approximately how many undersea species have been discovered in the world's oceans?

A 96,000—or the approximate human population of Shrewsbury, England

B 230,000—or the approximate population of Salina Cruz, Oaxaca, Mexico

C 680,000—or the approximate population of Bhutan

D 1.2 million—or the approximate population of Dallas, Texas

137. When one lobster loses a fight to another lobster, what does the losing lobster do?

Ⓐ Swims off and dies

Ⓑ Finds another, smaller lobster to fight

Ⓒ Steers clear of the winner in the future

Ⓓ Immediately seeks out food to replenish its energy

138. Several product designs have taken their cues from nature. Match the product—and the challenge it was designed to overcome—with the animal on which the solution is based.

The bullet train
Challenge: to reduce the thunderous claps from pressure changes as the train exits tunnels.

The boxfish, with its bony skin structure

The bionic car
Challenge: to create an aerodynamically efficient car without sacrificing safety or spaciousness.

The large, irregular bumps on the leading edge of humpback whale flippers

The wind turbine
Challenge: to lessen the noise generated by turbines and improve reliability in low wind.

The beak of the kingfisher, which dives smoothly into water

WEATHER AND NATURAL DISASTERS

You don't want to be caught in a tornado or tsunami, but they're compelling subjects from a safe distance. And the more details you know about lightning, earthquakes, and avalanches, the more fascinating they become.

139. TRUE OR FALSE?
Scientists at France's University of Lyon have discovered how to elicit lightning bolts on demand by firing laser pulses into a storm cloud.

140. The deadliest hurricane in U.S. history killed between eight and twelve thousand people in 1900. Where was it?

141. You've heard the term Tornado Alley. Which of the following groups of states are all part of this deadly territory?

Ⓐ Kansas, Texas, Oklahoma, and Colorado

Ⓑ Nebraska, Texas, Idaho, and Iowa

Ⓒ Minnesota, Texas, South Dakota, and North Dakota

Ⓓ Indiana, Missouri, Kansas, and Nebraska

142. What do changes in magma—the molten rock beneath the surface of a volcano—signal?

143. Which came first, the devastating flood of the Neva River in Russia or the even more devastating flood of the Yangtze River in China?

145. In its famous 1980 eruption, Mount St. Helens released thermal energy equivalent to 24 megatons of TNT in just a few moments. (FYI: a megaton is one million metric tons!) Was this release of energy more or less than that designed to be released by the Mark 36 strategic nuclear bomb?

144. The largest weather simulation tunnel in the world is in Vienna, Austria. It can create snow, sleet, intense heat, and humidity all in one day, and tests for safety, performance, and passenger comfort in cars, trains, and other vehicles. How long is the tunnel?

- Ⓐ **328 feet**—or the length of today's Erie Canal locks
- Ⓑ **756 feet**—or the length of the largest of the great pyramids
- Ⓒ **2,841 feet**—or the length of the record holder for the world's longest letter, which was written to God in 2010
- Ⓓ **3,221 feet**—roughly equivalent to the elevation of Lubbock, Texas

147. University of Florida researchers use a 10-foot-tall hurricane simulator to recreate a Category 3 hurricane. What's the most rainfall it produces per hour?

Ⓐ **8 inches**—or the height of a Tony Award

Ⓑ **13½ inches**—or the height of an Academy Award

Ⓒ **35 inches**—or the approximate height of the Stanley Cup

Ⓓ **44 inches**—or the height you must be in order to ride Space Mountain at Disney World

146. How many active volcanoes are there in the United States?

Ⓐ **3**—or the number of the kinds of alien encounters familiarized in Steven Spielberg's film

Ⓑ **26**—or the number of people who were crammed into a Mini Cooper to set a world record in 2011

Ⓒ **169**—or the number of medals won by India at the 2010 South Asian Games

Ⓓ **180**—or the number of episodes of *Seinfeld*

148. **TRUE OR FALSE?**
The space shuttle *Challenger* was not built with an escape system.

149. If you're in a car when a tornado approaches, what should you do?

Ⓐ **Get out and seek shelter indoors**

Ⓑ **Drive away**

Ⓒ **Get under the car**

Ⓓ **Lock the doors and duck**

150. The loose-snow type involves low cohesion among grains of snow. The slab type occurs when whole, bonded layers fracture and slide. The wind type involves a mixture of airborne crystalline and granular snow. These are types of what?

151. How fast are Category 5 hurricane winds on the Saffir-Simpson Hurricane Wind Scale, formulated in 1969?

152. In May 1889, days of rain in Johnstown, Pennsylvania, caused the collapse of the South Fork Dam, releasing 20 million gallons of water—roughly equivalent to the amount of Agent Orange the United States dropped on Vietnam. How many lives were lost at Johnstown?

Ⓐ **12**—or the number of people who have been to the moon

Ⓑ **103**—or the estimated number of people who traveled on the Mayflower

Ⓒ **1,509**—or the seating capacity of Broadway's Lunt Fontanne Theatre

Ⓓ **2,209**—or the approximate number of people named Thomas Roberts in the United States

153. The Fujita scale, which rates a tornado's wind speed, was replaced on February 1, 2007, with a new scale for measuring tornadoes. What is the name of the new scale?

154. **TRUE OR FALSE?**
Heavy volcanic ash can cause corneal abrasions.

155. The 1906 San Francisco earthquake registered 7.8 on the Richter scale. The 1989 Bay Area quake registered 6.9. The 7.8 quake released 22.4 times more energy than the 6.9 event. How is the Richter scale calculated?

A It is a base-2 logarithmic scale

B It is a base-5 logarithmic scale

C It is a base-10 logarithmic scale

D It is a base-20 logarithmic scale

156. Why do the wet winds blowing in on both sides of Florida make the peninsula a perfect place for a lightning lab?

157. How fast can the snow in an avalanche move?

ⓐ Up to 30 mph—or from the Hoover Dam to Las Vegas, Nevada, in an hour
ⓑ Up to 100 mph—or from Philadelphia, Pennsylvania, to New York City in an hour
ⓒ Up to 200 mph—or from Miami, Florida, to Cocoa Beach, Florida, in an hour
ⓓ Up to 400 mph—or from Cedar Point Amusement Park in Sandusky, Ohio, to Holiday World and Splashin' Safari in Santa Claus, Indiana, in an hour

158. TRUE OR FALSE?
Approximately 60 percent of New Orleans, Louisiana, was flooded in the wake of Hurricane Katrina.

159. Avalanches occur mostly on slopes of what degree?

ⓐ 10 to 15 degrees
ⓑ 25 to 50 degrees
ⓒ 60 to 70 degrees

160. In 2009, Siberia's Sayana-Shushenskaya Dam exploded. Put the following dam elements in order, from reservoir to outflow.

Control gate
Intake
Turbine
Penstock

161. What percentage of tsunamis originate in the Pacific Ocean?

163. TRUE OR FALSE?
The reason high winds cause lightning has to do with the way ice and hail move inside the eye wall of a thunderstorm.

162. Each year, 73,000 flights pass above one of the most volcanic areas on Earth. How many volcanoes in this area does the Alaska Volcano Observatory monitor?

Ⓐ 50—or the number of points Michael Jordan scored in three consecutive games against different teams

Ⓑ 80—or the number of days it took fictional Phileas Fogg to circumnavigate the Earth in Jules Verne's classic novel

Ⓒ 110—or the statistically impossible percentage of effort that coaches often encourage their players to give

Ⓓ 160—or the optimal temperature, in Fahrenheit, to which ground beef should be heated before it is safe to eat

SURVIVAL

Sometimes a little knowledge can keep you from being a late story on the evening news. How much do you know about surviving avalanches, floods, and other calamities?

164. TRUE OR FALSE?
You should rub snow on frostbite.

165. The chance of survival for a person buried in an avalanche plummets after how long?

166. You're in the desert and you need water to survive. You see a small pool of water, but it looks scummy. Should you drink it or not?

167. TRUE OR FALSE?
The typical person, lost in the wilderness, can live for weeks off body fat.

168.

What percent chance do you have of surviving a lightning strike?

169. What is the main cause of death for victims buried by an avalanche?

170. TRUE OR FALSE?

If you're stuck outdoors during a lightning storm, you should try to get into a hardtop vehicle.

171. Rank the following places to go from most to least desirable in the event of a tornado.

A mobile home

The interior part of basement

The first-floor room near a piano

A bedroom on the first floor

A windowless bathroom

172. It happened to New Orleans—and it could happen in other places, too. Each of these cities is vulnerable to being crippled by water. Match the city to the reason.

Houston, Texas	Built on a flood plain, which could be overrun by rain and meltwater from nearby mountains
London, England	Only 13 feet above sea level
Sacramento, California	Poor drainage with easily flooded underground tunnels
St. Petersburg, Russia	Tilts further toward the southeast by 2 feet per century

173. TRUE OR FALSE?

If the branches or twigs you plan to use for your fire feel cool when you place them next to your cheek, they're too wet to burn efficiently.

174. When preparing for an emergency—a hurricane, quake, or other disaster—you need to stockpile water for each member of your family. How much water should you reserve per person per day?

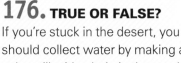

175. You are free-falling from 22,000 feet. Roughly—okay, very roughly—how long do you have until impact?

Ⓐ Thirty seconds
Ⓑ One minute
Ⓒ Two minutes
Ⓓ Three minutes

176. TRUE OR FALSE?
If you're stuck in the desert, you should collect water by making a solar still with a hole in the sand, a sheet of plastic, and the drip, drip, drip of condensation into a pot.

177. Fill in the blanks for survival.
You can live three minutes without _____,
three hours without _____,
three days without _____,
and three weeks without
_____.

178. For how long can a person survive in 40°F water?

CHAPTER 3

TOOLS

You can't do your work without your tools, and your tools won't work unless you use them properly. But how well do you actually know the finer points of pliers? The nuts and bolts of screwdrivers? The ins and outs of drills? See if you can nail these challenging questions.

UNDER THE HOOD

If the tool-to-square feet ratio in your house is approaching critical mass, these are the questions for you.

179. Abrasives are rated by what?

Ⓐ Coating
Ⓑ Pounds per square inch
Ⓒ Grain size
Ⓓ Tsubo mineral density

180. The coarse, chisel-like teeth of this handsaw are effective in cutting parallel with the grain. What is it?

181. What does an ABC fire extinguisher use as a propellant?

182. What do old-fashioned stud finders use to find drywall screws?

183. How many people are injured by chain saws each year?

Ⓐ 12,000—or about the same number of people who entered the San Jose Thanksgiving Turkey Trot in California in 2010

Ⓑ 24,000—or about the number of registered Hajj pilgrims in Thailand in 2011

Ⓒ 36,000—or the estimated number of people killed by the Krakatoa volcano eruption in Indonesia in 1883

Ⓓ 48,000—or the estimated number of people who attended the 2007 Burning Man festival in Nevada's Black Rock Desert

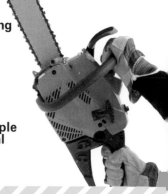

184. There are two kinds of routers: the fixed-base design that handles edge molding, dadoes, and rabbets, and the plunging version that's best for internal cuts. Which came first?

186. Discs for random-orbit sanders are of two mounting types. Which *isn't* one of these types?

Ⓐ Pressure-sensitive adhesive
Ⓑ Hook-and-loop
Ⓒ Rough top

185. The Pulaski is a tool used in fighting wildfires. Of what two tools is it comprised?

187. Which two of the following tools did the original Fu-Bar combine?

Ⓐ A hammer
Ⓑ A wrench
Ⓒ A pry bar with serrated jaws
Ⓓ A funnel

188. What kind of wood is usually used as the handle of a handsaw?

190. **TRUE OR FALSE?**
LED flashlights are more efficient than incandescent models by as much as 90 percent.

191. For blacksmiths, low-carbon steel is fine for most projects, but high-carbon steel is better for shaping implements that need to hold an edge. Low-carbon steel contains approximately 0.05 to 0.15 percent carbon. How much does high-carbon steel contain?

189. In his efforts to rebuild a twin-engine Heinkel He-219 Uhu aircraft, Will Lee of the Smithsonian National Air and Space Museum used four dozen of what tool?

Ⓐ Saws   **Ⓑ** Metal files   **Ⓒ** Wrenches   **Ⓓ** Pliers

Constantly upgrading and improving your tool arsenal? While your set of combination wrenches may not be tucked away in a felt-lined box, this could be the section for you.

192. What's the best tool for removing—in one piece—a mirror that's glued to a wall?

A A putty knife
B Cutout wire
C A chisel
D Wire snips

193. When using a circular saw, should you have the best surface of the board facing up or down? (Bonus: why?)

194.

The drill you're using to punch a hole through the floor is stopped dead by a large knot. Where does all that torque go?

195. Match the compound-action snip (aka aviation snip) to its color-coded handle.

Yellow	**Right-hand curves**
Red	**Combination cuts**
Green	**Left-hand curves**

198. **TRUE OR FALSE?**
Phillips-head screwdrivers are designated by numbers, and the larger the number, the larger the tip and the lighter the screw it's designed to drive.

196. How far should the blade of a circular saw extend past the edge of the board you are cutting?

197. You are a painter. You've got a knife. Actually, you have multiple knives. Match the use to the blade.

Chisel-edge putty knife	**Spreading drywall compound, patching cracks, light scraping**
Flexible 4-inch knife	**Touching up putty or drywall compound on painted surfaces without leaving scuff marks**
Painter's tool	**Scraping loose paint, lifting small pieces of wallpaper, removing crumbling window putty, decal removal**
Disposable knife	**Cleaning excess paint off rollers, scraping paint, and raking failed caulk out of siding and trim or weeds from sidewalk control joints**

199. What material is a bull point chisel designed for?

A Concrete
B Stone
C Brick
D Wood

When possible, use a screw with an exposed head.

201. You need to grip all six flats of a nut. Which wrench do you use?

A An open-end wrench
B A flare-nut wrench
C A box-end wrench
D A ratcheting box wrench

202. Match the type of pliers with its primary use.

Long-nose	Gripping pipe, plumbing fittings, and oddly shaped parts such as broken bolts
Tongue-and-groove	Cutting wire in a tight spot
Diagonal cutters	Cutting copper wire and bending hooks in wire to fit over terminal screws

203. Match the drill bit to its use.

Framing lumber, beams, and logs

Sheet metal, metal boxes, 1/8-inch flat and L-shaped steel or aluminum

Standard and pressure-treated lumber

Anything but masonry, glass, or tile

Step drill

Ship auger

Twist drill

Spade bit

204. The letters A, B, and C on a fire extinguisher denote what type of fire it will put out. Match each letter with the type of fire it extinguishes.

A   An electrical fire

B   Flammable liquids such as grease, oil, and gasoline

C   Ordinary combustibles such as wood and paper

205. For every 4 feet the ladder goes up the wall, how far from the wall should you place the ladder's base?

206. TRUE OR FALSE?
Screws will drive more easily if you lubricate the threads with wax.

207. You've set up a ladder against your house to clean your gutters. At what angle should it tilt?

A **25 degrees**—or the angle of descent into the largest burial chamber of the Pyramid of Khafre, Egypt

B **50 degrees**—or the degree of the 120-foot drop on the Talon roller coaster at Dorney Park in Allentown, Pennsylvania

C **75 degrees**—or the angle between two hands of a clock at 8:30

D **80 degrees**—or the angle of the hole that was to be drilled as part of Plan B to rescue trapped Chilean minors in 2010

208. Put these tools in order from the most aggressive to the least aggressive rust remover.

Disc sander
Wire brush
Palm sander
Sandpaper
Grinder

209. Congratulations! You've successfully magnetized the tip of your screwdriver. But now you want to demagnetize it. What's a quick and easy way to do this?

210. TRUE OR FALSE?

Using a shorter screw will make up for a less-than-perfect pilot hole and boost grip.

211. Which of the following is an alternate use for a center punch?

A Tightening a loose handle on a knife

B Marking a wood line on wood or metal

C Countersinking a large nail head

D All of the above

213. Which tool is *not* used to finish concrete?

A A float

B An edger

C A level

D A groover

214. TRUE OR FALSE?

For heavy work with a saw, you can increase the cutting speed by switching to a saw with more teeth per inch.

212. There are many tried and true tools for removing a stuck fastener. Can you name five different tools that can help you out of a tight spot?

NAME THAT TOOL

Remember when you got your first peek into your father's tool box, and all the questions you had? These are much tougher.

215. This little tool comes in handy when marking an even reference line around a room. Just put it on a level surface and rotate it. What is it?

216. This handy tool operates with about 1,400 inch-pounds of torque—tripple what a drill/driver puts out—without delivering that torque to the handle. What is it?

217. The sanding area on a belt sander is under a rectangular pad called a...

Ⓐ Platen
Ⓑ Workpiece
Ⓒ Abrasive disc
Ⓓ None of the above

218. For some, it's Turfgrass Producers International. For others, it's Timber Products Inspection. But when you've got a crosscut saw with a TPI of nine, what does that abbreviation stand for?

219. Name the three basic types of power sanders.

220. Which of these clamps doesn't exist?

Ⓐ A frame clamp
Ⓑ A wooden cam clamp
Ⓒ A solar clamp
Ⓓ A fast-acting clamp

221. You'll always know how to use an ABC fire extinguisher if you remember P-A-S-S. What does PASS stand for?

222. Match the punches and sets with what they're made for.

Automatic center punch

Nail set

Center punch

Tapered drift punch

Marking hole positions in hardened steel and cast iron

Driving out assembly pins

Rapid, repeated marking of hole centers in wood and metal

Setting nail heads

223. What kind of tool do in-the-know firewood splitters use?

A An ax   **B** A maul

C A hatchet   **D** An awl

224. Which term below is not the name of a router bit?

A Chamfer   **B** Cover

C Ogee   **D** Quarter-round

225. Match the description of the tape with its name.

Synthetic rubber compounds, carbon black, granular filler on peel-off backing

Wax paper with adhesive bead

Fiber-reinforced plastic (7.7 to 12.6 millimeters thick) with rubber or synthetic rubber adhesive

Vinyl or PVC (7 to 8.5 millimeters thick) with adhesive that ranges from mildly to extremely sticky

Silicone rubber (20 to 30 millimeters thick) with peel-off backing

Crepe paper (4.5 to 5.5 millimeters thick) with rubber or acrylic adhesive

Crepe paper (5.7 to nearly 8 millimeters thick) with rubber adhesive

Duct

Self-fusing rubber

Electrical

Electrician's putty

Glue strip

Masking (painting and heavy-duty)

Masking (general)

CHAPTER 4

TRANSPORTATION

Want to make friends? Be the person who knows how to get a nonworking vehicle rolling again. (Either that, or be the one who owns the truck.) This next quiz focuses on planes, boats, trains, cars, and other vehicles that get you—or your payload—from point A to point B.

FIX-IT-YOURSELF

Say the word *mechanics* and most people will immediately think of automotive repair. How many of these questions can you answer without relying on the guy at the shop in the grease-stained coveralls?

226. There are three sizes of blade-style fuses for your car. Which of these isn't one of them?

Ⓐ Mini
Ⓑ Average
Ⓒ Normal
Ⓓ Maxi

227. If your windshield wipers stop working, what is the first thing you should check for?

228. TRUE OR FALSE?
You should ask your neighbor to periodically idle the engine of the car you've left in your driveway during your extended vacation to keep it primed for your return.

229. To dispose of brake fluid, what should you do?

Ⓐ Use it for weed control
Ⓑ Mix it with used motor oil
Ⓒ Leave the container open until it dries
Ⓓ All of the above

230. Why are they called two-stroke engines?

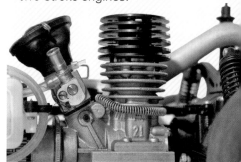

231. Something smells nasty. Match the offense to the likely cause.

The Smell

Ⓐ Gym socks when you turn on the heater or air-conditioner fan

Ⓑ Burnt carpet after you've been using the brakes a lot, or hard, or both.

Ⓒ Maple syrup after the engine has warmed

Ⓓ Rotten eggs when the engine is running

The Cause

❶ Coolant is leaking.

❷ Hydrogen sulfide is not converting to sulfur dioxide in the catalytic converter.

❸ Mildew growing in the moisture condensing inside your air conditioner's evaporator

❹ The brake pads are overheated.

232. What are the three things that keep the camshaft on a DOHC or V-type OHC engine and crankshaft in sync?

....

233. TRUE OR FALSE?
The best way to install a car cover is to lay it on one end of the car and pull it over.

234. TRUE OR FALSE?
You can save gas by putting your modern fuel-injected car in neutral when going downhill.

235. There's a sticker on the fender you bought that says "CAPA." What does that mean?

Ⓐ It comes from the Central American Parts Association, an organization of manufacturers based in Mexico City, Mexico.

Ⓑ The California Academy of Parts Administrators has approved its condition.

Ⓒ Its fit and finish standards of manufacture have been guaranteed by the Certified Automotive Parts Association.

Ⓓ It's been part of a test study by Computer Assisted Parts Analysis.

236. What can cause bent valves?

Ⓐ Over-revving the engine

Ⓑ A timing belt that has slipped a few teeth

Ⓒ A camshaft chain that has slipped a few teeth

Ⓓ Foreign objects that have found their way into the intake

Ⓔ All of the above

237.

What do most vehicles use to hold open liftgates, hatches, trunk lids, and engine compartment hoods?

238. TRUE OR FALSE? Restarting the engine uses more gas than idling.

239. What is the average life span of a brake lining in a modern car driven in urban conditions?

Ⓐ 8,000 miles—or the distance of the 2012 Olympic torche's travels around the United Kingdom

Ⓑ 10,000 to 15,000 miles—or about the distance from Tokyo, Japan to Toronto, Canada and back (not that we would recommend driving that route)

Ⓒ 15,000 to 20,000 miles—or about the distance from Alaska to Argentina

Ⓓ 20,000 to 25,000 miles—or roughly the circumference of the Earth

240. How many moving parts does your car's oxygen sensor have?

A **Five**—or the same number of moving parts there are in a Zeroshift transmission

B **Four**—or the same number of moving parts as there are in a Jonova engine

C **Two**—or the same number of moving parts as there are in Bourke engine

E **None**—or the same number of moving parts as there are in an Einstein refrigerator

241. You just replaced your rearview mirror and parked your car in the shade. Why was this a good idea?

242. Why is it usually a better idea to replace your wiper blades rather than cleaning them with solvent?

243. The high-frequency pulsations of this cleaning device make it a bad choice for use on your car or truck tire sidewalls. What is it?

244. TRUE OR FALSE?
Most cars with an automatic transmission can be safely flat-towed.

245. When is your car's traction poorest?

246. Your steering wheel shakes at all speeds. When you steer the car is slow to respond, and its response is not accurate. What's the problem?

Ⓐ A tire is out of round due to uneven wear or internal damage.

Ⓑ At least one wheel is bent, most likely from hitting a curb or pothole while going a little too fast.

Ⓒ A wheel is loose.

Ⓔ Your tires were rotated improperly.

247. When should you check tire pressure?

Ⓐ When the tires are cold, first thing in the morning

Ⓑ When the tires are warm, first thing in the morning

Ⓒ When the tires are warm, late in the day

Ⓓ When the tires are cold, late in the day

248. TRUE OR FALSE?
Worn-out tie-rod ends will make your steering inconsistent and your front tires wear out rapidly.

249. When you start a car with fuel injection, should you pump the gas pedal?

250. You've patched a radiator hose, and you're ready to crank the engine. Check the radiator level first. If it's low and you don't have a can of coolant or water handy, what can you fill it with?

Ⓐ Diet soda
Ⓑ Regular soda
Ⓒ Fruit juice
Ⓔ All of the above

251. The "check engine" light has come on. Where should you plug in the scan tool to get a code?

252. TRUE OR FALSE?
Your daughter just left for college for four years and no longer needs her car. Putting it in storage is your best bet.

253. What is a possible cause of fan belt failure?

Ⓐ Misaligned pulleys
Ⓑ Rubber buildup in the grooves
Ⓒ A worn-out tensioner spring
Ⓔ All of the above

254. What should you lube a key tumbler with: graphite or penetrating oil?

Before you change your car's oil, you should warm up the engine to stir up any sediment in the crankcase.

256. What is the correct ratio of coolant-to-water in coolant mix?

257. You could only afford a pair of new tires instead of four. Assuming all are equally worn, what is your best move?

A Install the new tires in back and move the two best old tires to the front.

B Install the new tires in the back and leave the front tires alone.

C Install the new tires in the front and leave the rear tires alone.

E Install the new tires in the front and put the old tires in the back.

258. TRUE OR FALSE? Tire pressure changes 1 psi for every 1 degree of outside temperature, with pressure going down as the temperature drops.

259. When your mechanic investigates a short underneath the hood, he may insert the probe of the multimeter in the back side of the socket to make the connection, instead of in the front. What is this technique called?

261. You need to jump-start your car. Do you use the red cable to connect the batteries' positive or negative terminals?

260. TRUE OR FALSE? When the paint job on your car begins to chip, this provides a toehold for rust to begin. You will want to fix these right away.

262. While plastic-and-aluminum car radiators aren't worth fixing, others made out of this metal can almost always be repaired. What is it?

263. TRUE OR FALSE?
If you find your car plunging into a lake (or river or ocean), you should lower the window the moment your car hits the water.

264. Your car blows a tire. What should you do?

265. TRUE OR FALSE? When changing a tire, tighten the nuts in a circular pattern.

266.

Which way should you turn the steering wheel when parking on a hill?

Ⓐ Turn it all the way to the curb.
Ⓑ Turn it all the way to the street.
Ⓒ Turn it as far as you can in either direction.
Ⓔ Don't turn it at all.

267. Your car has broken down in a deserted area. You need help. What is the international sign for distress?

268. TRUE OR FALSE?
When storing your car long term, you should remove its battery.

269. You can find tire-pressure information on a sticker on your car's door frame, in the owner's manual, and printed on the tire sidewall. These won't agree. Which should you ignore?

270. Which of the materials below can you safely use to dry your car after you've washed it?

Ⓐ A chamois towel
Ⓑ A terrycloth towel
Ⓒ A microfiber towel
Ⓓ Any of the above

271. You've got a leak in your radiator, and you're stranded miles away from help. What can you use to plug the hole for a while?

Ⓐ A raw egg
Ⓑ Gum
Ⓒ A stick
Ⓓ Densely packed soil

BEHIND THE WHEEL

Autopilot won't cut it for these tough car questions. But you might be able to improve your car's mileage.

272. Today's cars still have a bumper, but it's hidden. Where is it located?

273. TRUE OR FALSE?
Millions of cars in the United States are outfitted with little black box data recorders—like the black boxes in planes that are scrutinized after a crash.

274. NASCAR Sprint cup cars share two features with standard automobiles. Which two? (Bonus: which feature is found only in your car?)

A Four-wheel disc brakes
B Computer-controlled ignition timing
C Safety fuel cell
D Power-assisted steering

275. How many barrels of crude oil are required to produce enough gasoline to power a Honda Civic from New York to California?

Ⓐ **Four**—or the number of kippered herring barrels containing the Marx Brothers in *Monkey Business*

Ⓑ **Five**—or the number of a different kind of barrels in a Nerf Lightning Blitz toy gun

Ⓒ **Ten**—or the number of pins in a standard bowling lane

Ⓓ **Twenty**—or the number of barrels of blood in Neil Young's song "Vampire Blues"

276. **TRUE OR FALSE?**
Ethanol used for fuel is made using the same process that produces moonshine.

277. Which has a faster reaction time—the brain stem and motor cortex of a human, or the electronic control unit of an automobile?

278. You know that sitting in the middle of the backseat of a car is safer—at least 16 percent safer—than other seats. How much safer is it than sitting shotgun?

Ⓐ Up to 28 percent safer
Ⓑ Up to 50 percent safer
Ⓒ Up to 64 percent safer
Ⓓ Up to 86 percent safer

279. Modern tractor-trailers come equipped with some of the most advanced tracking and safety features on the road. What feature don't they have?

Ⓐ Satellite tracking
Ⓑ Lane-departure warning
Ⓒ Cargo sensors
Ⓓ Wind sensors and stabilizers

280. In what year were antilock brake systems (ABS) introduced?

Ⓐ **1970**—the year Al Unser won his first Indy 500
Ⓑ **1971**—the year Al Unser won his second Indy 500
Ⓒ **1978**—the year Al Unser won his third Indy 500
Ⓓ **1987**—the year Al Unser won his fourth Indy 500

281. TRUE OR FALSE?

In 2006, Honda made a Civic GX sedan with an exhaust system that produced exhaust cleaner than the air in some high-pollution areas.

282. Truckers in Canada's Northwest Territories cross frozen lakes in their rigs. How thick does the ice have to be to support the heaviest trucks?

A **15 inches**—or the thickness of the deck of the Jordan River Dam on Vancouver Island

B **25 inches**—or the length of the world's largest potato chip in the Idaho Potato Museum

C **40 inches**—or the length of the lens in what, in 1897, was the world's largest telescope

D **100 inches**—or the average annual snowfall in Lander, Wyoming

283. TRUE OR FALSE?
You should fill your gas tank with premium fuel every few tankfuls.

284. TRUE OR FALSE?
When your car is stuck in mud, sand, or snow, you should gun the engine to get out.

285. What is the key to clean diesel?

A Ultra-low-sulfur fuel
B Ultra-high-sulfur fuel
C More saturated hydrocarbons
D Fewer saturated hydrocarbons

286. The U.S. automotive recycling industry reclaims about how many pounds of scrap every month?

Ⓐ 100 million pounds—or the amount of asphalt used to resurface the Daytona International Speedway in 2011

Ⓑ 500 million pounds—or the approximate amount of rice imported by Indonesia in 2010

Ⓒ 750 million pounds—or the amount of hazardous waste a court ordered the United Steel Mills plant in Haifa, Israel, to clean up in 2010

Ⓓ 900 million pounds—or the amount of domestic steel construction in Vietnam in 2010

287. How fast must cars in National Highway Traffic Safety Administration front-crash tests be going (plus or minus 2/10 mph) at the time of impact?

Ⓐ 35 mph—or the estimated speed at which molasses poured into the streets of Boston, Massachusetts in the Great Molasses Flood of 1919

Ⓑ 50 mph—or the top speed of a wildebeest

Ⓒ 80 mph—or the highest posted speed limit in the United States

Ⓓ 90 mph—or the speed that souped-up golf carts have reached

288. TRUE OR FALSE?

Diesel and gasoline engines are both internal combustion engines designed to convert the chemical energy in fuel into mechanical energy.

289.
Physics lets us predict the way an exhaust system will affect performance. What are the real variables? Pick two.

A The length and diameter of the pipes

B The length and diameter of the oxygen sensor

C The length and diameter of the mufflers

D The length and diameter of the catalytic converter

290. TRUE OR FALSE?

Most gasoline now contains some ethanol.

291.
Household wiring is AC. What is car wiring?

....

292.
What is another name for fishtailing: oversteering or understeering?

293. There are three antiknock indexes: RON, MON, and AKI. What does each of these fuel rating systems stand for?

294. **TRUE OR FALSE?** The rubber seal in the cap on the end of the tire stem is what keeps the air from leaking out of your tire.

295. Which has more moving parts, a pair of hydraulic brake calipers or the Murchison Widefield Array (MWA) telescopes in Australia?

296. About how many gallons of excess gas are burned every year as a result of underinflated tires?

Ⓐ 100 million—or the estimated amount of oil lost in Mexico's 1980 spill

Ⓑ 740 million—or the estimated amount of jet fuel used during flight delays in 2008

Ⓒ 1.2 billion—or the approximate amount of potable water used in New Jersey each day

Ⓓ 2.2 billion—or the amount of sewage transported annually through the Newark, New Jersey, sewer system

297 How much spare change is found in scrapped vehicles, on average?

Ⓐ 11 cents
Ⓑ 26 cents
Ⓒ $1.65
Ⓓ $4.05

300. **TRUE OR FALSE?**
Most alloy wheels are painted silver, then clear-coated, so you should treat them like any other painted surface.

298. Which megavehicle has a greater horsepower engine, the Caterpillar 797B six-wheel-drive dump truck or the Oshkosh Striker 4500 eight-wheel-drive aircraft rescue fire fighting apparatus?

301. Five different technologies are used in automotive telematics—the systems that allow for automatic roadside assistance and remote diagnostics. Name three of them.

299. Who financed the 1979 Budweiser Rocket Car, which may or may not have broken the sound barrier (the debate continues)?

Ⓐ Stuntman and *Smokey and the Bandit* film director Hal Needham
Ⓑ Chuck Yeager
Ⓒ The French government
Ⓓ Donald Trump

302. The 1933 Blue Bird got up to 272 mph on Daytona Beach. Why couldn't it go any faster?

Ⓐ The driver panicked.
Ⓑ There was insufficient traction.
Ⓒ Sand built up in the motor.
Ⓓ None of the above.

303. TRUE OR FALSE?
Modern cars can overheat while idling.

304. In 1904, the Ford 999 reached a then-record 91.37 mph. Who was the driver?

Ⓐ Count Jules-Albert de Dion
Ⓑ René Panhard
Ⓒ Thomas Flyer
Ⓓ Henry Ford

305. An engine needs three of the following to start. Which of the items below is not needed?

Ⓐ Fuel
Ⓑ Oil
Ⓒ A spark
Ⓓ Compression

306. Which auto manufacturer almost was destroyed by a 1986 *60 Minutes* report about unintended sudden acceleration?

Ⓐ **Audi**
Ⓑ **Mazda**
Ⓒ **Fiat**
Ⓓ **Ford**

307. TRUE OR FALSE?
The Ford Motor Company built 308,000 Model T's in 1914 alone—which was 100,000 more cars than the rest of the entire American auto industry.

308. TRUE OR FALSE?
Unlike gasoline, diesel fuel can grow bacteria.

309. Datsun was created in 1931 (and originally spelled Datson). In what year did Nissan eliminate the brand?

Ⓐ **1976**—or the same year Ford introduced the Fiesta
Ⓑ **1982**—or the year Honda's first U.S. factory started rolling
Ⓒ **1986**—or the same year Chevrolet stopped manufacturing the Chevette
Ⓓ **1989**—or the year Lexus launched its first model

PLANES, TRAINS, AND BOATS

You don't need to know how to operate a plane, train, or boat to answer these questions, but you do need to have a boatload of information about topics ranging from airplane design to train engines. Can you keep your answers on track?

310. What percentage of an airliner's takeoff weight is fuel?

A 5 to 10 percent
B 10 to 15 percent
C 15 to 25 percent
D 25 to 45 percent

311. The U.S. Navy's X-Craft is a littoral, high-speed aluminum catamaran. What does littoral mean?

312. What does the elevator on the rear of an airplane control?

A Pitch
B Roll
C Yaw
D All of the above

313.

The Breguet Range Equation states that the distance an airplane can fly is determined by three factors. Which of these isn't one of them?

A The efficiency of its power plant

B Its lift-to-drag ratio

C Its wing weight

D Its fuel fraction (the percentage of its takeoff weight that is fuel)

---

314. Between 2002 and 2007, how many fatal commercial airline crashes occurred in the United States?

315. Every airplane design starts with what?

A The engine

B The cockpit

C The wings

D The tail

316. Sailboats participating in the round-the-globe Volvo-sponsored ocean race sport high-tech features and nifty designs. For example, their retractable daggerboards prevent leeway (sideslipping) by providing lateral force (lift) when the keel is canted. The daggerboards are painted bright orange. Why?

317. What are the "spoilers" on an airplane?

318. Match the following aviation milestones to the year in which each occurred.

Orville Wright pilots the *Wright Flyer* in a twelve-second flight.	1905
Gabriel Voisin takes off over the Seine in a box kite glider towed by a motorboat.	1920
The first international balloon race takes place, beginning in Paris, France and ending in North Yorkshire, England.	1903
The first flying club, the Aeronautical Society of New York, is founded.	1910
Mademoiselle Elise Deroche becomes the first licensed female pilot.	1908
The first wireless airship-to-ship message is sent.	1906

319. Which class of submarines is not designed for deep-ocean combat?

A Los Angeles **B** Seawolf
C Virginia **D** Ohio

320. How many gallons of paint are required to cover the rubber-coated polyester exterior of the Goodyear blimp?

Ⓐ 26 gallons—or the amount of bottled water consumed by an average American family in 2011

Ⓑ 53 gallons—or the size of a bourbon barrel

Ⓒ 98 gallons—or the approximate monthly gas purchase for a two-car family

Ⓓ 140 gallons—or the amount of water required to produce a gallon of milk

321. Airlines often attach upturned winglets to a plane's wingtips. Why?

322. Roughly what percent of all U.S. freight moves by train?

323. What percent of global carbon dioxide emissions do airplanes produce?

324. The Federal Aviation Administration (FAA) lists several rules for ultralight aircraft used for entertainment or sport purposes. Which is not one of the FAA's rules?

Ⓐ A top speed of just over 60 mph

Ⓑ One occupant limit

Ⓒ A 5-gallon gas tank

Ⓓ A weight of less than 254 pounds

325. Pilots are responsible for looking out the cockpit window to make sure they're not about to collide with another plane. What is this doctrine called?

326. Approximately how many miles of track are used by U.S. freight trains?

A **90,000 miles**—or a little more than the entire coastline of the United States

B **140,000 miles**—or the equivalent of one thousand trips from Gettysburg, Pennsylvania to Philadelphia, Pennsylvania

C **240,000 miles**—or about the distance from Earth to the moon in miles

D **500,000 miles**—or the amount of mileage you need to receive lifetime benefits as part of Korean Air's Morning Calm Premium Club program

327.

Your plane is about to take off. Put the following organizations in the order in which they guide your plane from takeoff until you start your descent.

Air route traffic control centers

Air traffic control towers

Terminal Radar Approach Control (TRACON)

328. Freight trains are how many times more fuel efficient than trucks?

Ⓐ Three times—or as many times as Lionel Ritchie believes his love is "a lady"

Ⓑ Five times—or the number of times John Gotti was arrested between 1957 and 1961

Ⓒ Ten times—or as many times as Taiwan could fit into Japan

Ⓓ Twelve times—or the number of times builder Ian Burston was brought back to life by a Welsh ambulance staff after suffering a heart attack.

329. About 5 percent of the world's ocean cargo passes through the Panama Canal each year. About how many vessels does that translate to?

ⓐ **6,000**—or the age of a wine-making facility found by archeologists in Armenia

ⓑ **8,000**—or the number of miles four driverless vans traveled from Italy to China in 2010

ⓒ **14,000**—or the number of white boxes in sculptor Rachel Whiteread's 2005 installation at the Tate Modern gallery in London, England

ⓓ **27,000**—or the number of players who signed up for the first PokerStars Spring Championship of Online Poker in 2009

330. You've heard of maglev trains that zip through Japan, China, and elsewhere at hundreds of miles per hour. What does maglev stand for?

331. TRUE OR FALSE?
A Boeing 747 moves 500 mph faster than a Fuji blimp.

332. The U.S. Navy uses colors to describe where a ship is built to operate. Match the color to the body of water.

Brown	Oceans
Blue	Coastal waters
Green	Only Regional Operation

333. What is the name of the largest U.S. warship?

334. What is the gunwale of a canoe?

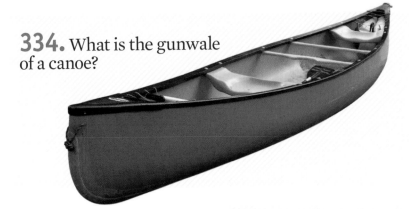

335. Which has the right of way: a sailboat or a powerboat?

336. In canoeing, what is the name of the start of the blade's pull through the water?

337. How many gallons of fuel does a 747 burn while idling one hour, waiting for takeoff?

- **Ⓐ 500 gallons**—or the amount of water that an E-One/Spartan fire truck can hold
- **Ⓑ 1,000 gallons**—or the amount of gas stolen from a Gualala, California, Chevron station in April 2011
- **Ⓒ 2,000 gallons**—or the amount of water that a medium-size tree can filter in a year
- **Ⓓ 3,000 gallons**—or about the amount of water needed to fill a 12-foot round aboveground swimming pool

338. How fast do jets travel per minute?

A **9 miles per minute**—in an hour, that's the distance from Lexington, Kentucky, to Charleston, South Carolina

B **20 miles per minute**—in an hour, that's the approximate distance between Durango, Mexico, and Durango, Colorado

C **48 miles per minute**—in an hour, that's the approximate distance between Tucson, Arizona, and Bangor, Maine

D **64 miles per minute**—in an hour, that's the approximate distance between Juneau, Alaska, and Jersey City, New Jersey

339.

Where is the motor for maglev trains?

340. What is the top speed of the Shinkansen, the Japanese bullet train?

341. How much does the Shinkansen weigh?

A **100 tons**—or the estimated amount that superhero Iron Man can lift

B **300 tons**—or the weight of the Mars candy bars stolen by Martin Keys in 1998

C **500 tons**—or the weight of the steel capstone at the top of the San Francisco Bay Bridge tower

D **700 tons**—or the weight of one of Egypt's Colossi of Memnon stone statues, created in 1350 BC

342. The nuclear-powered *USS George Washington*, capable of carrying eighty-five planes, can steam for a long time before refueling. Exactly how long?

Ⓐ Eighteen days—or the time it took for Hosni Mubarak to resign as president of Egypt after protests began
Ⓑ Eighteen weeks—or the length of many college semesters
Ⓒ Eighteen months—or as long as it took to shoot the puppet-animation film *Coraline*
Ⓓ Eighteen years—or the number of years of Jesus' life not accounted for in the four Gospels

343. UAVs are remote-control spy planes used in warfare. What does UAV stand for?

344. Pilots carry electronic flight bags that plug into the cockpit navigation system. What are they?

345. One type of UAV has a 26-hp two-stroke engine that gives it a modest cruising speed. How fast does it go?

Ⓐ 40 mph—or about the maximum speed of a zebra
Ⓑ 60 mph—or about the speed of a pronghorn antelope
Ⓒ 90 mph—or about the speed of a homing pigeon
Ⓓ 170 mph—or about the diving speed of a peregrine falcon

346. Catapults on the flight deck of an aircraft carrier launch F-14 Tomcats from 0 to 130 mph in how many seconds?

Ⓐ 2.5 seconds—or the amount of time a target is shown during the fast-run Olympic shooting event

Ⓑ 9.58 seconds—or the record set by Usain Bolt in 2009 for the fastest 100 metre-dash

Ⓒ 12 seconds—or the duration of Orville Wright's first powered airplane flight

Ⓓ 21 seconds—or the time it took Chicago Blackhawk Bill Mosienko to score three goals in his record-setting 1952 game against the New York Rangers at Madison Square Garden

347. Why does the U.S. military want its armored vehicles to emit little or no heat?

348. The U.S. Air Force Reserve's Fifty-third Weather Reconnaissance Squadron is the only group in the world directed to do what?

CHAPTER 5

HOME DIY

Home is where the heart is, goes the old saw. It's also, as any homeowner knows, where most of the work is. Here's a chapter full of questions that test your knowledge of home repair and improvement. Proceed with caution if you are puzzled by plumbing, dumbfounded by drywall, or confused by concrete.

HANDYMAN SPECIAL

If you're a competent handyman or woman, the Honey-Can-You list will grow exponentially. How much do you really know about practical painting or tackling a leaking toilet?

349. You are finally painting your living room. After you dip the roller in the paint tray, what percent of the paint comes off on the first downstroke?

350. Your toilet comes on by itself, runs for a bit, then shuts off. Most likely, it's a problem with what part?

351. Which roll of sealant tape—the yellow or the blue spooled one—do you use to seal the gas pipes on your dryer?

352. TRUE OR FALSE?
You can remove water from a toilet by pouring water into it.

353. It's a tough call. You've already made your decision to change the siding on your house, and you've chosen to use wood for the job. You like the look of cedar shingles, but the expert at the lumber liquidation outlet suggests you take a look at another kind. It is hand-split with a steel-bladed froe, then sawed in half to create a rough surface and a flat, smooth back. What is it?

354. After painting, at what angle should you remove any masking tape to avoid lifting paint while peeling up the tape?

- **A** 90 degrees
- **B** 45 degrees
- **C** 20 degrees
- **D** Straight up

355. You think you have a leak in your toilet, so you put a few drops of food coloring in the tank. Why would you go and do a thing like that?

356. TRUE OR FALSE?
Plastic electrical boxes need to be grounded.

357. Your faucet is leaking and you want to ignore it, but you know that every drip is costing you money. How much will a drop a second cost you in wasted hot water per month? (National average.)

- **Ⓐ $1**
- **Ⓑ $5**
- **Ⓒ $10**
- **Ⓓ $15**

358. Name the four ingredients that, when mixed together, make concrete.

359. You've got a plumbing problem. The galvanic connection between your copper and galvanized steel pipes has corroded. Your solution: replace it with a fitting that uses a steel collar on the steel side, a copper collar on the copper side, and isolation bushing to keep the two apart. What's another name for this union?

360. Which common household product can help you loosen rust and mineral deposits on a plumbing job?

- **Ⓐ Coca-Cola**
- **Ⓑ Toothpaste**
- **Ⓒ Hairspray**
- **Ⓓ Milk**
- **Ⓔ All of the above**

361. You're a snowbird, and you're leaving your house for the winter. Assuming you have no pets, how low can you safely set the thermostat while your house is unoccupied for an extended period?

Ⓐ 36°F—or the amount by which trees in Davis, California, parking lots reduced asphalt temperatures

Ⓑ 50°F—or the water temperature around which crappies (a species of freshwater fish) leave their deep-water shelters

Ⓒ 60°F—or the water temperature at which largemouth bass begin to spawn

Ⓓ 90°F—or the temperature at which you should keep a basking spot for your pet Chinese water dragon

362. You've just come back from an extended vacation to discover a foul odor in your bathroom. Yes, the drain trap dried and let in sewer gas. What's the easy fix?

363. What is the most common type of electrical box?

Ⓐ Single-gang box
Ⓑ Octagon box
Ⓒ Switch box
Ⓓ Square box

364. Bathrooms in older homes are notoriously ill-equipped for the power demands of hair dryers and other modern gadgets. To avoid dimming lights, tripped circuits, or dangerous overheating, what is the minimum number of amps a bathroom's dedicated circuit should have—especially in a home that contains teenage girls?

365. Your clothes dryer needs a new exhaust duct. You know enough to upgrade from the cheap plastic one. But what kind of duct is best?

366. GFCI protection is required in any potentially wet situation. It safeguards against the chance of electrocution. What does GFCI stand for?

367. You just replaced a windowpane. Before painting, should you let the putty dry for:

Ⓐ 60 minutes (as in the name of the long-running CBS series)

Ⓑ Three days (as in the time in the title of that *Condor* movie)

Ⓒ Two weeks (as in the amount of notice needed in the title of a 2002 Sandra Bullock movie)

368. You want to insulate your attic to reduce heat loss. What kind of insulation should you install if you plan to turn the attic into an office or a bedroom?

369. You've got water. You've got a clean cotton cloth. You've got an iron. How can you, MacGyver, fix a dent in wood?

HOW THINGS WORK

There's something deeply satisfying about knowing you can rise to the challenge, whether it's demolishing an old front stoop or caulking the tub. But do you know why your tools and materials perform the way they do?

370. You've just emptied a 24-ounce can of traditional spray foam insulation. Maybe you did it to make your home more energy efficient. Maybe you did it as a prank. Whatever the case, the result was somewhere in the neighborhood of 19 gallons of foam. Does that number sound about right?

371. You've installed a ceiling fan and plan to use it year round to mix air layers with different temperatures, making the room more comfortable. In winter, the air will be forced up to help raise the temperature in the occupied area of the room. How do you know in which direction the air will be forced?

372. What's the maximum number of watts your microwave needs to meet most normal household needs?

Ⓐ 100 to 300 watts
Ⓑ 300 to 500 watts
Ⓒ 500 to 800 watts
Ⓓ More than 800 watts

373. Which is greater, the number of times a dimmer turns a light off per second, or the age of telephone inventor Alexander Graham Bell when he died?

374. Pressure-washer capacity is measured in cleaning units, or the product of water pressure (in psi, or pounds per square inch) multiplied by flow rate (in gpm, or gallons per minute). A bare bones electronic pressure washer operates at about how many cleaning units?

Ⓐ 1000 **Ⓑ** 1600
Ⓒ 2400 **Ⓓ** 3200

375. The R-value is the value of the resistance heat meets as it moves through a material. An inch of foam insulation can have an R-value of 7. What is the R-value of an inch of wood?

376. If your refrigerator is running, it requires this many watts to keep your food fresh.

- **Ⓐ** 100 to 200 watts
- **Ⓑ** 300 to 400 watts
- **Ⓒ** 500 to 700 watts
- **Ⓓ** 800 to 1000 watts

377. In screenwriting, *VO* means voiceover. To a history buff, *VC* refers to the Vietcong. And we all know that a VCR is a videocassette recorder—even if none of us owns one anymore. But when it comes to painting, there's something called low-VOC, which purports to take the stench out of redecorating and the chemicals out of the environment. In this case, *VOC* stands for volatile organic *what*?

378. Which came first, the patenting of galvanization or the first publication of Nathaniel Hawthorne's *The Scarlet Letter*?

381. TRUE OR FALSE?
The farthest switch and receptacle cables can be stapled from electrical boxes is 1 foot.

379. Which is greater, the typical inlet water pressure in a home or automobile tire overpressure?

380.

When two or more dissimilar metals come together under moist conditions, galvanic corrosion is likely to occur. One of the best-known victims of such corrosion has been the...

Ⓐ Parthenon
Ⓑ Atlantic City boardwalk
Ⓒ Statue of Liberty
Ⓓ Astrodome

382. How quickly does air in a forced-air heating system move through the house?

Ⓐ About 7 feet per minute—the average speed of a three-toed sloth

Ⓑ About 70 feet per minute—the high end of a mole's speed through tunnels

Ⓒ About 700 feet per minute—the top speed for the Sky Ride in the Otis Elevator exhibit at the 1933–34 Chicago World's Fair

383. What color should the flame be in your water heater?

384. Why is it a really bad idea to run your generator in an enclosed garage?

385. How is the water heater's recovery rate—the rate at which the heater can raise the temperature of the inlet water by 90°F—measured?

Ⓐ By gallons per hour

Ⓑ By degrees per hour

Ⓒ By gallons per minute

Ⓓ By degrees per minute

386. Do the two heating elements in your electric water heater come on at the same time or sequentially?

387. TRUE OR FALSE?
Modern furnaces rely on a fan to create a draft up the chimney.

388. What three materials (none of them wood) are most homes in developed countries constructed out of?

389. Chimney flashing serves three purposes. Which purpose doesn't it serve?

Ⓐ Accommodating movement between the roof and the chimney.
Ⓑ Protecting the house from lightning strikes.
Ⓒ Protecting the joint against leakage from rain or melting snow.
Ⓓ Sealing the joint between the roof and the chimney.

390. TRUE OR FALSE?
Wet concrete is strongly alkaline and can cause a chemical burn if it contacts bare skin.

391. TRUE OR FALSE?
In ideal conditions, light-colored roof shingles can reflect summer heat, saving up to 20 percent on air-conditioning costs.

393.
Lumber sizes are nominal dimensions of rough-hewn lumber in inches. After the wood is planed, it's smaller. All two-by lumber is 1½ inches thick. How wide is a two-by-four?

394.
What is the nickname for engineered cementitious composites (ECCs)?

392. Between what temperatures does concrete cure best?
Ⓐ **30° and 50°F** (March in New York, New York)
Ⓑ **50° and 70°F** (December in Orlando, Florida)
Ⓒ **70° and 80°F** (July in Iowa)
Ⓓ **80° and 90°F** (year-round in the Costa Rican lowlands or the temperature range that attracts ants—take your pick)

395. There are three types of toilets—besides "seat up," "seat down," and "broken." Which kind below isn't one of them?

Ⓐ Gravity flow
Ⓑ Pressure-assist
Ⓒ Silent-flush
Ⓓ Suction-drain

396. TRUE OR FALSE?
You can lose about 100 Btu of heat per hour per square foot of floor space if you have no insulation and loose-fitting doors and windows.

....

397. You've got a draft blowing into your house at 7 mph. In addition to causing a chill, it's degrading the R-value of your fiberglass insulation by what percent?

Ⓐ About 10 percent
Ⓑ As much as 40 percent
Ⓒ Between 50 and 60 percent
Ⓓ More than 60 percent

398. What is the difference between caulk and sealant?

399. Window and ceiling fans use only a small percentage of the energy that a central air conditioner unit uses. But let's get more specific: how small of a percentage?

400. The tendency of a window to let heat pass is described as its what?

Ⓐ K-factor
Ⓑ H-factor
Ⓒ U-factor
Ⓓ Max Factor

401. Fill in the blanks:

Floors are supported by heavy beams called _____ . These sit on _____ anchored to the foundation with galvanized metal straps or 1/2-inch L-bolts.

402. Standard electrical receptacles are rated at how many amps?

Ⓐ 5 or 10
Ⓑ 15 or 20
Ⓒ 25 or 30
Ⓓ 45 or 50

CONSTRUCTION KNOW-HOW

Should you have called a contractor before tackling the big job yourself? If you can answer the following questions correctly, you might be able to take them off speed dial.

403. "Hey," says your know-it-all father-in-law, "you've got 200 amps' worth of circuit breakers in a 100 amp panel box." Did he catch you making an electrical mistake?

404. Portland cement plaster is an alias for what?

405. What percentage of a typical gallon of latex paint is water?

A **15 percent**—probably the amount of your last water rate hike

B **50 percent**—about the amount of water in your engine coolant

C **65 percent**—about the amount of water in the average human

D **80 percent**—equivalent to the percentage of water in an orange

406. Some hardwoods treat more easily than others. Rank the following from easiest to hardest to penetrate.

American sycamore
Cottonwood
Red oak
White oak

407. Which of these woods has the longest life expectancy if untreated?

Ⓐ Ash
Ⓑ Northern white cedar
Ⓒ Douglas fir
Ⓓ Maple

409. There are three main components in a typical staircase. Which of the components below isn't one of them?

Ⓐ Stringers   Ⓑ Decking
Ⓒ Treads   Ⓓ Risers

408. You're building a monument in your backyard that will be one thousand steps high. Assuming you are working with the average rise per step, will your building be taller than the Washington Monument?

410. It will take six bags of concrete mix to make 1 cubic yard of concrete. But how much mix would you need if you wanted to cover a 2-yard-by-2-yard area, or 4 cubic yards?

412. Pencil-thick tubes snaking along joists may mean what kind of trouble?

411. How well do you know your drywall? Match the type of drywall to the job (but always check your local building codes first).

Standard ¼-inch	Serves as a tile backer on bathroom ceilings
Standard ½-inch	Covers walls and ceilings in an attached garage or in the room above
Standard ⅝-inch	Covers walls and ceilings framed on 16-inch centers
Fire-resistant ⅝-inch	Serves as a tile backer on bathroom walls
Water-resistant ½-inch	Covers cracks
Water-resistant ⅝-inch	Covers walls and ceilings framed on 24-inch centers

413.

You're mixing concrete, and you've reached the final step: adding just the right amount of water. Of course, the phrase "just the right amount" is a decidedly unscientific one. Let's get a little more specific. You want it to be the consistency of what?

A Paint
B Peanut butter
C Window cleaner
D Milk

414. You've got a roll of paper tape and a roll of fiberglass mesh tape. Which should you use for producing neat seams in a drywall project?

415. The first generation of skylights had an airspace sealed between their panes of glass for insulation. What do modern skylights use for insulation?

416. Biscuits aren't just for breakfast anymore. They're also used for mating boards. What are these kind of biscuits?

417. TRUE OR FALSE?
When taping drywall, the wider the band of compound, the smoother the joint.

418. You've bought a box of nails that claims they're "HD Galv," meaning they are...

419. You are considering buying a fixer-upper and notice uneven spaces around the doors and windows. Besides a less-than-qualified builder, what could this indicate?

420. Tuck-pointing is...

- **A** The process of removing crumbling and deteriorated mortar from between bricks and replacing it with fresh mortar
- **B** Cutting and fitting woodwork to an irregular surface
- **C** The second-to-last stage in concrete work
- **D** A safety control that shuts down a furnace

421. What length does most crown molding come in?

- **A** 1-foot lengths
- **B** 4-foot lengths
- **C** 8-foot lengths
- **D** 16-foot lengths

422. You're assembling frames and cabinet panels with a technique called toenailing. Besides wondering who comes up with such names, what are you doing?

423. Does a spinning circular saw blade enter through the top or the bottom of the wood you are cutting?

424. Match the wire with its official name.

Hot wire

Neutral wire

Grounding wire

Ungrounded conductor

Grounded conductor

Equipment-grounding conductor

425. What is the "spline" you encounter when replacing a damaged screen?

Ⓐ The narrow rubber tubing that locks a screen in a groove around the frame

Ⓑ The frame around the screen

Ⓒ The mesh in the screen

426. A skylight is usually installed in one of two ways: above the roof deck on a small curb or set into the deck. Which method is best used on shallow roofs?

427. Joe and Jack are replacing siding. Joe drives the nail heads all the way down. Jack doesn't. Which one knows what he is doing?

428. How much does a sheet of regular ½-inch drywall weigh per square foot?

Ⓐ .6 pounds

Ⓑ 1 pound

Ⓒ 1.7 pounds

Ⓓ 2.2 pounds

429. TRUE OR FALSE?
Dedicated circuits, like those serving dishwashers or bathrooms, can't be extended.

430. TRUE OR FALSE?

In most cases, if a wall's plane is perpendicular to the rafters, ceiling joists and floor joists, it's load-carrying.

432.
The most common way to frame a house is with wood. And the simplest wood framing is known as stick framing. But there are two types of stick framing. One is platform framing. What is the other, older method called?

431. TRUE OR FALSE?

A double-glazed window is about twice as efficient in keeping in heat as a single-glazed window. You can therefore conclude that a triple-glazed window is about three times as efficient as a single-glazed window.

433.
Match the filler with what it's best-suited for.

Spackling paste	Concealing nail holes and minor surface blemishes
Colored wood putty	Odd jobs, repairing metal, or resetting hardware on knockdown furniture
An epoxy stick	Rebuilding painted wood architectural elements, such as windowsills
Epoxy-based wood filler	Filling small cracks and minor dents in wood, masonry, and metal

YARD WORK

You have to live with the results of your less-than-successful interior projects, but your neighbors will have to live with the exterior missteps. Before you begin, how much do you really know?

434. You know that if you step on a crack, you could cause a life-threatening spinal cord injury to your maternal parent. But what is the joint where two panels in a concrete walks meet actually called?

435. Which type of softwood lumber is better for outdoor projects: flat grain or vertical grain?

436. TRUE OR FALSE?
When cleaning aluminum siding, you should wash from the top down.

437. You have a loose piece of copper step flashing where the roof and sidewalk meet. After the neighborhood association writes you a third threatening letter, what kind of nail should you use to secure it?

Ⓐ Aluminum
Ⓑ Copper
Ⓒ Steel
Ⓓ Any nail will do

438. A well-designed gutter system should carry roof runoff at least how many feet from the foundation wall?

Ⓐ **1 foot**—or the height of architect Aldo Rossi's *Tea and Coffee Piazza*

Ⓑ **4 feet**—or the title of a poem by Rudyard Kipling

Ⓒ **10 feet**—or how far west the city of Concepción, Chile, moved as a result of the 2010 earthquake

Ⓓ **23 feet**—or nearly the world record for the women's long jump

439. To prevent an ice dam, keep the underside of a roof deck below what temperature?

Ⓐ **10°F**—or the average winter temperature in Minneapolis, Minnesota

Ⓑ **30°F**—or the temperature at which Arctic seawater freezes

Ⓒ **60°F**—or the average temperature at the beginning of spring in South Dakota's Badlands National Park

Ⓓ **95°F**—or the normal body temperature of an opossum

440. This one wasn't your fault—not completely. You left a garden hose in a bucket of sudsy water. Meanwhile, a car plowed into a fire hydrant in front of your house. The result is backflow. The sudsy water is pulled through the hose and into the municipal water system. Unlikely, yes, but what attachment to your hose (required by some municipalities) could have prevented the backflow?

441. A roof square equals how many square feet?

Ⓐ 10 square feet—or the minimum amount of recommend coop space per pet chicken (if you have no outdoor run space)

Ⓑ 35 square feet—or the common minimum standard for the amount of space needed per kid in a child-care classroom

Ⓒ 100 square feet—or the size of a hotel room at New York's Pod Hotel

Ⓓ 130 square feet—or the approximate size of a compact car parking space in the United States

442. When wood is stacked to the depth of one stick of wood, it's known as all of the following except what?

Ⓐ A face cord
Ⓑ An oven cord
Ⓒ A furnace cord
Ⓓ A rick

443. It seems logical to use concrete to seal a crack in a house's foundation. Water-stopping mortar is better for the job, though. Why?

444. There's a diseased tree in your front yard that needs to be removed. The first step is a first cut. But should that be on the side facing where you want the tree to fall or on the opposite side?

445. A traditional gable roof is composed of what rigid geometric shapes?

Ⓐ Squares
Ⓑ Rectangles
Ⓒ Triangles
Ⓓ Diamonds

447. How far should the lower edge of a roof extend beyond the fascia board?

Ⓐ It shouldn't extend beyond the fascia board at all.
Ⓑ At least ¾ inches
Ⓒ 2 inches or more

446. Match the style of roof to its definition.

Gable	A symmetrical roof found in Dutch Colonial houses, with two slopes on each side
Gambrel	A Victorian-style four-sided roof with two slopes on each side, the upper less steep than the lower
Mansard	An asymmetric roof with one side topping a second story and the other sloping down to top the first floor on the other side
Saltbox	A roof whose edges extend over the wall, as in classic Cape Cod houses

CHAPTER 6

SPACE

The moon landing of July 20, 1969, was the culmination of thousands of years of human fascination with all things beyond the earth's atmosphere. How much do you know about man's journey to the stars?

MAN IN SPACE

The act of ascending to the stars is complex: spacecraft contain many moving parts and missions require detailed planning and extremely precise calculations. Can you guess the answers to these stellar questions?

448. Approximately how many satellites (factoring out the unknown number of spy satellites) are currently circling Earth?

449. What year was the space shuttle's first mission?

450. The Chandra telescope uses as much power as what?

Ⓐ A General Motors factory
Ⓑ A hair dryer
Ⓒ A dishwasher
Ⓓ A shopping mall

451. What is the Hubble Space Telescope primarily searching for in the sky?

452. The *Columbia* shuttle disaster initiated the largest debris search in history. More than eighty-four thousand pieces of the shuttle were recovered. What percentage of the shuttle does that constitute?

453. How much did the Hubble Space Telescope cost?

Ⓐ **$1 billion**—or the amount that Baghdad asked the United States to pay to cover damage done after the second Gulf War

Ⓑ **$2 billion**—or the top figure for the amount of damage the U.S. Geological Survey says is caused annually by mudslides

Ⓒ **$3 billion**—or the value of the Los Angeles Dodgers' twenty-year broadcast agreement with Rupert Murdoch's News Corporation, proposed in 2011

Ⓓ **$4 billion**—or the approximate cost of the damage done in the U.S. by Hurricane Isabel in 2003

454. The Hubble Space Telescope is the closest thing we have to...

Ⓐ A time machine
Ⓑ The most powerful super-computer ever known
Ⓒ A giant digital camera
Ⓓ All of the above

455. In 2005, *Voyager 1*, the probe launched to explore the outer planets of our solar system, broke through the termination shock to the terminal region of the solar system, where solar wind gives way to interstellar gases. What is another name for this area?

456. Match the space agency with the year it was formed.

The National Aeronautics and Space Administration (NASA)	1958
The Russian Aviation and Space Agency/ The Russian Federal Space Agency	1992
The European Space Agency (ESA)	1973
The Canadian Space Agency (CSA)	1989
The Japan Aerospace Exploration Agency (JAXA)	2003
The China National Space Administration (CNSA)	1993

457. NASA normally replaced about one hundred damaged thermal protection system tiles after each shuttle flight. For Discovery, in 2005, how many tiles did NASA replace?

A 73—or David Seidler's age when he won an Oscar for writing *The King's Speech*. (He commented that he was a late bloomer.)

B 690—or the year the Dome of the Rock was built

C 1,900—or the year of the first automobile show in the United States

D 4,800—or the age of the bristlecone pine, considered the oldest currently living organism

458. Where is the Arecibo Observatory, home of the world's largest radio telescope, located?

A Arizona
B Puerto Rico
C New Mexico
D Brazil

459. No vehicle runs forever. What was the expected driving distance of the Martian rover *Spirit*?

460. What is the name of the telescope at the Paranal Observatory in Chile?

A The Very Large Telescope
B The Large Binocular Telescope
C The Paranal Telescope
D The Mapuche Telescope

461. Name all five Mars exploration rovers.

462. When astronauts are in space, they do not experience a twenty-four-hour light cycle. How many hours per day (on average) do they sleep?

463. If you hit a golf ball from the International Space Station, how long would it orbit the Earth before being pulled into the atmosphere?

464. How far did the *Spirit* rover actually travel before it stopped transmitting in March 2010?

465. Who was the first tourist in space?

466. When Russian cosmonaut Pavel Vinogradov was planning to hit such a golf ball (in a stunt that was eventually canceled), from what was the intended club made?

A Yttrium
B Titanium
C Scandium
D Vanadium

467. What are the first and second top nonmilitary schools in graduating future astronauts?

A The Massachusetts Institute of Technology (MIT) and Purdue University
B MIT and the California Institute of Technology (CIT)
C CIT and MIT
D CIT and Michigan State University

468. How many pounds of lunar material did NASA retrieve during the Apollo missions?

Ⓐ 72 pounds—or nearly the weight of the 2008 record-setting world's largest meatball

Ⓑ 276 pounds—or the approximate weight of an adult panda

Ⓒ 590 pounds—or the amount of pounds per foot of torque generated by a 2011 Mercedes Benz CL 63 AMG sedan

Ⓓ 837 pounds—or approximately the weight of the Bahia Emerald

469. The Soviet *Zond 5* made the first round-trip moon orbiting mission with a payload of what?

Ⓐ Turtles
Ⓑ Empty boxes
Ⓒ Newspapers
Ⓓ Apples

470. The space shuttles were originally designed for one hundred flights each, and at one point NASA envisioned sixty missions per year. What was the highest number of missions the shuttles actually flew in a calendar year?

471. What is the name of the fifth and final shuttle, first launched in 1992?

472. As the 2003 *Columbia* accident so tragically demonstrated, a spacecraft's TPS is a matter of life and death. What does TPS stand for?

473. TRUE OR FALSE?
Amazon.com founder Jeff Bezos owns a spaceship.

474. What was the name of the first space probe to orbit Saturn (in 2004) ?

Ⓐ Cassini
Ⓑ Rosetta
Ⓒ Voyager
Ⓓ Pioneer

475. How long did it take that probe to orbit Saturn to reach the planet?

476. What was the name of the chimp sent to space in *Mercury* in 1961?

477. What is the name of the first satellite launched by the United States in 1958?

478. What is aerobraking?

479. What is the record for most consecutive days spent in space, set in 1995?

Ⓐ 212

Ⓑ 438

Ⓒ 643

Ⓓ 819

480. Giant radio telescopes are moved around New Mexico's remote Plains of San Agustin high desert by a telescope transport that boasts a 400-horsepower, six-cylinder Cummins diesel engine with 1,000 pound-feet of torque. What is the top speed of this mover?

Ⓐ 3 mph—or the top speed of an American cockroach

Ⓑ 27 mph—or approximately the fastest speed attained by a human on foot

Ⓒ 44 mph—or the approximate top hopping speed of a red kangaroo

Ⓓ 60 mph—or the speed a Volkswagen Barabus TKR can reach in 1.67 seconds

481. What piece of his spacesuit did Neil Armstrong leave on the moon?

482. What was the diameter of Sputnik 1?

483. How quickly does the Lunar Reconnaissance Orbiter spin around the moon in 2009?

Ⓐ 1,200 mph—or the highest wind speed clocked on Neptune, our solar system's windiest planet

Ⓑ 2,600 mph—or the speed that, in the 1950s, Lewis Flight Propulsion Laboratory scientists believed that their turbojet engine could help airplanes to reach

Ⓒ 3,600 mph—or the speed reached by a V-2 rocket in 1946

Ⓓ 4,500 mph—or the jaw-dropping approximate wind-speed clocked on the planet HD 209458 b, which is 150 light-years from Earth

484. In what year did the first manmade probe leave the solar system?

485. The parachute for the NASA Mars Science Laboratory rover, scheduled to reach the Red Planet in August, 2012, opens to a diameter of 52 feet, making it twice the size of any parachute ever flown beyond Earth. How much does it weigh?

Ⓐ 20 pounds—or the average amount of fruit that a semi-dwarf olive tree will bear in a season once it reaches maturity

Ⓑ 44 pounds—or the average weight of a king cobra snake

Ⓒ 86 pounds—or the weight of the heaviest turkey ever raised

Ⓓ 120 pounds—or the weight of each anvil fired 200 feet into the air by the former world champion anvil shooter, Gay Wilkinson

486.

At what altitude does NASA recognize aviators as astronauts?

487. GPS is a system consisting of how many satellites (plus several orbiting in reserve)?

488. What is the destination of the *New Horizons* spaceship, launched in 2006?

489. What is the name of the first communications satellite?

490. Which Mars lander first performed the tests that confirmed the existence of water on Mars in 2008?

491. TRUE OR FALSE? In the International Space Station, urine is converted into clean water via a recycling system.

492. The Chandra X-ray Observatory is named after Nobel scientist Subrahmanyan...

Ⓐ Chaudhary   **Ⓑ** Chandragupta
Ⓒ Chandresekhar   **Ⓓ** Chauchesku

A BRIEF HISTORY OF THE UNIVERSE

From supernovae to asteroids:
how much do you know about these
heavenly bodies?

493. What is the name of the 525-foot-wide, 65-foot-deep depression just south of the Martian equator?

Ⓐ Southern Crater
Ⓑ Endurance Crater
Ⓒ Tranquility Crater
Ⓓ Apollo Crater

494. How many asteroids have single moonlets—small, natural satellites—that orbit the asteroid?

495. On which planet (other than Earth) was the first hurricane-like storm with a well-defined eye and eye wall spotted in 2006?

496. To which planet does the moon Hyperion belong?

497. How many years ago did primitive galaxies begin to form?

Ⓐ **Five billion**—or about the number of seconds in 155 years

Ⓑ **Eight billion**—or the amount, in dollars, made in the U.S. box office by comic book movies in 2010

Ⓒ **Thirteen billion**—or the approximate amount, in dollars, of the United States national deficit in 1900

Ⓓ **Twenty billion**—or the number of tweets sent through social media powerhouse Twitter as of July 2010

498. Scientists believe an invisible substance makes up about 85 percent of all matter in the universe. What is it called?

499. Approximately how many tons of interplanetary material drift to Earth's surface on a daily basis?

Ⓐ 10 tons—or the weight of the Clothespin statue in Philadelphia, Pennsylvania

Ⓑ 50 tons—or the weight of the MGM Lion statue in Las Vegas, Nevada

Ⓒ 100 tons—or the weight of Buddha Shakyamuni statue at the Bai Dinh Temple in Vietnam

Ⓓ 200 tons—or the weight of the statue of the god Tlaloc in Mexico City, Mexico

500. Astronomers keep looking for potentially habitable planets. What quality is *not* required for a planet to be habitable?

Ⓐ A relatively low mass

Ⓑ Water

Ⓒ Orbits close enough to a star for a warm, life-supporting climate

Ⓓ A molten center

501. Which two planets in our solar system do not have moons?

502. TRUE OR FALSE?
Asteroids are composed mostly of water, ice, and rock and are formed in the cold outer solar system beyond the planets' orbits.

503. Match the moon to its planet.

Saturn	Triton
Jupiter	Phobos
Mars	Ganymede
Neptune	Titan

504. Fill in the blanks. There is one common thread to life on Earth that scientists know for certain: all life here is composed of the same basic building blocks.

All proteins are made of *compounds* known as

_____.

All genes are made of *molecules* known as

_____,

which are attached to a *backbone* made of _____

and a *sugar* called _____.

505. How do scientists determine the temperature of the surface of the sun?

Ⓐ By measuring patterns of vibrations that indicate fusion reactions powerful enough to generate high temperatures

Ⓑ By analyzing the color of the visible light emitted by the sun

Ⓒ By measuring the radiation streaming from the core of the sun

Ⓓ By comparing the gravitational effects of the sun on the inner planets

506. TRUE OR FALSE?
More than 1,000 planet candidates have been discovered outside of our solar system.

509.
A standard 1,500-watt space heater can easily warm your living room. Would it take more or less than a billion space heaters to artificially warm Earth by 1.08°F?

507.
What 1958 invention can be used to repair a broken taillight, reassemble a vase, close wounds, and lift fingerprints?

508.
What is the name of the first impact crater ever identified on Earth (which is also the best preserved)?

Ⓐ The Chesapeake Bay impact crater
Ⓑ The Popigai impact crater
Ⓒ The Sudbury basin
Ⓓ The Barringer crater

CHAPTER 7

SPORTS

From baseball to the biathlon, and from football to curling, the wide world of sports offers athletes endless opportunities for competition and camaraderie. This section offers you the opportunity to show off your extensive knowledge of sports. Are you game?

We've come a long way from those first Olympics in Greece. How well do you know the rules of these games?

510. Joseph-Armand Bombardier invented the Ski-Doo in 1937. What's the more common name for this vehicle?

511. Indy 500 engines used to run on methanol. What do they run on now?

512. A NASCAR driver will go through several tires during a race. How many tires will a driver on the smoothest track use?

513. What world championship "car" race is held every August at Derby Downs in Akron, Ohio?

514. While performing the butterfly stroke, what kind of acid tends to build up in swimmers' muscles, reducing their ability to swim faster?

515. What percentage of tennis pros' first serves are successful?

517. TRUE OR FALSE? In professional football, the quarterback has a microphone in his helmet so he can talk to his head coach.

518. A NASCAR engine costs $50,000 to build. How many races will it last?

516. How long is the Iditarod, which takes place annually in Alaska?

- **A** **210 miles**—or the approximate distance from Nashville, Tennessee, to Memphis, Tennessee
- **B** **800 miles**—or the approximate distance from Chicago, Illinois, to New York, New York
- **C** **1,100 miles**—or the approximate distance from Green Bay, Wisconsin, to Baton Rouge, Louisiana
- **D** **1,600 miles**—or the approximate distance from Roswell, New Mexico, to Orlando, Florida

519. How long does a batter have to stop his 2-pound bat in time to check the swing?

Ⓐ 10 milliseconds—or the threshold at which subliminal messages become invisible to the naked eye

Ⓑ 50 milliseconds—or the amount of time it takes to form an opinion about a website, according to a paper published in the journal of *Behaviour & Information Technology*

Ⓒ 80 milliseconds—or the amount of time it took the MythBusters to paint a replica of the Mona Lisa using coordinated paintball guns

Ⓓ 110 milliseconds—or the half-life of the isotope nickel-78

520.

Cyclists in most races ride close to the lead rider to benefit from his windbreak, but cyclists in the Ironman World Championship must keep a certain distance from each other. How far is that distance?

521. Who is the head coach in the Super Bowl talking to on his headset?

Ⓐ All his assistants on the sidelines

Ⓑ The defensive coordinator

Ⓒ The running backs' coach in a box above the game

Ⓓ All of the above

522. Which is safer for a NASCAR driver: a prolonged crash or one that ends in a moment?

523. What is the optimum distance your feet should be apart for the perfect push-up?

524. Which of the following NASCAR tracks is not made of concrete?

Ⓐ Tennessee's Nashville Superspeedway

Ⓑ Tennessee's Bristol Motor Speedway

Ⓒ The Michigan International Speedway

Ⓓ Delaware's Dover International Speedway

525. Match the top speed of the sphere to the Olympic sport.

Volleyball	155 mph
Shot put	about 65 mph
Tennis ball	70 mph
Ping pong ball	30 mph
Water polo ball	about 82 mph
Soccer ball	112 mph

526. Topwater hard lures for fishing include three of the four lures below. Which one doesn't belong here?

Ⓐ Buzzbaits
Ⓑ Poppers
Ⓒ Crankbaits
Ⓓ Chuggers

527. Downhill skiers can choose to use short or long skis. Which generate more speed?

528. How fast must the 3 meter diving board project an Olympic swimmer upward for him or her to reach a height of at least 18 feet above the water?

Ⓐ 5.3 mph—or the speed at which king and chinstrap penguins have been recorded swimming

Ⓑ 12.3 mph—or the maximum speed of a Bobcat S630 skid-steer tractor/loader

Ⓒ 22.3 mph—or the top speed reached by wheelchair racer David Weir in the 2011 IPC Athletics World Championships

Ⓓ 31.3 mph—or the speed a 2010 Toyota Prius III can reach in pure zero-emissions mode

THE SCIENCE OF SPORTS

Do you know why a curveball curves?
There's real science behind these games.
Let's see how you shape up.

529. Researchers rate a field's shock absorbency with a metric called G-Max. A low G-Max means the field absorbs more energy than the player. Which has a higher G-Max in football fields: grass, synthetic turf, or frozen grass?

530. What kinds of vehicles are entered into the DARPA Grand Challenge?

531. British anthropologists, analyzing the results of boxing, tae kwon do, and wrestling at the 2004 summer Olympics, found that contestants dressed in which color were more likely to win their bouts?

Ⓐ Black
Ⓑ Blue
Ⓒ Red
Ⓓ Yellow

532. Golf ball manufacturers were asked to make their products less efficient in response to increasingly longer drives. Which rollback wasn't considered?

A "Unlinking" the molecular structure of the polybutadiene-based core for less efficient energy transfer

B Softening the mantle so the ball regains its round shape less quickly

C Injecting the ball with pellet-size weights

D Reverting to prior dimple configurations, increasing drag

533. The University of Phoenix Stadium—home to the Arizona Cardinals—features a 108,000-square-foot field of natural grass that can be moved outside the roofed stadium on rails for the sunlight it needs to grow. How long does it take the grass to move in and out of the stadium?

A 15 minutes—or the amount of time it took seven thousand people in the Philippines to plant 64,096 trees in 2011

B 45 minutes—or the time it took Jesse Owens to tie the world record in the 100-yard dash *and* set the world record in the long jump, the 220-yard dash, and the 220 low hurdles

C 79 minutes—or the length of the longest song yet recorded, "Mind Control Experiment" by Kiol Xeno, Rob Prescott, and Cory Estouteville

D 90 minutes—or the amount of time that the Pee Battery managed to stream 1.5 volts using human urine

534. Which can be hit farther: a curveball or a fastball?

535. What percent of a pole vaulting pole's length should bend when it is planted?

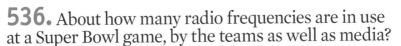

536. About how many radio frequencies are in use at a Super Bowl game, by the teams as well as media?

A **290**—or the number of calories in a hamburger kids' meal from Burger King

B **500**—or the approximate number of calories in a McDonald's strawberry shake

C **1,200**—or the possible calorie count in a Chipotle Mexican Grill—depending on how heavily you pile on the guacamole

D **1,800**—or the amount of calories that could be in your Johnny Rockets bacon cheddar double hamburger

537. The NBA briefly replaced leather basketballs with balls made of a different material. These new basketballs bounced more erratically than the leather ones—and also bounced about 5 percent lower—so the NBA returned to leather. What was the different material?

538.

In pitching, what is a gyroball?

//

539. What is the top wind speed at the Penske Technology Group's wind tunnel, where engineers test NASCAR models?

A **80 mph**—or the approximate speed bungee jumper Rishi Baveja was traveling when his harness worked loose and he hit the river Thames in 2009. (He recovered after a month in the hospital.)

B **110 mph**—or the speed world champion motorcyclist Michael Doohan was going when he crashed during qualifiers for the 1999 Spanish Grand Prix. (He broke his wrist, leg, and collarbone.)

C **180 mph**—or the speed actor and racecar driver Jason Priestley was travelling when he hit a wall at the Kentucky Speedway in 2002. (He fractured his spine, broke his nose, and had broken bones in both feet.)

D **210 mph**—or the speed passed by two-time Daytona 500 champ Bill Elliott in 1987 before horsepower-lowering restrictor plates were made mandatory by NASCAR.

540. TRUE OR FALSE?

The g-load (here the g stands for "gravitational") of a shuttle launch is 3.0, while the g-load of an extreme football impact is 30.

541. In 2005, the 2.5-mile Indianapolis Motor Speedway track was milled and repaved for the Indy 500. How many tons of asphalt, applied in two layers, did it take to do the job?

A **8,000 tons**—or the approximate amount of trash generated during 2010's Mardi Gras in New Orleans, Louisiana

B **18,500 tons**—or the weight of the bricks, mortar, and steel used in what, in 1910, was the world's tallest smokestack in Great Falls, Montana

C **28,000**—or the weight of the *USS New York*, a dreadnaught-class U.S. Navy ship built in 1911

D **38,000 tons**—or the amount of horse meat produced in Mongolia every year

542. Improvements to NASCAR track walls have made crashes safer for drivers. What were the walls made of before these improvements?

544. TRUE OR FALSE?
A batter facing a 90-mph fastball takes about 150 milliseconds to swing his bat.

543. The challenge in bobsled racing is akin to that of NASCAR racing: designing a vehicle that can go slightly faster, while staying within fraction-of-an-inch official specs. A NASCAR racecar's top speed is approximately 200 mph. What is a bobsled's approximate top speed?

Ⓐ **85 mph**—or the speed limit proposed in Texas in 2011
Ⓑ **110 mph**—or the record-setting speed of hockey player Denis Kulyash's slap shot
Ⓒ **140 mph**—or the top speed of a British Rail Class 91 locomotive
Ⓓ **160 mph**—or the sustained wind speed of Super Typhoon Choi-Wan in 2009

545. Approximately how far do physicists estimate a man could hit a ball, at sea level, without help from the wind?

A **475 feet**—or the height above sea level of the municipality of Magé, the lowest point in Brazil's Serra dos Órgaõs National Park in Brazil

B **725 feet**—or the height above sea level of Lewiston, Idaho's lowest point

C **1,100 feet**—or the approximate elevation of Lake Mead at the Hoover Dam (which was at just 708 feet in 1935)

D **1,400 feet**—or the approximate elevation of Lakeside, Iowa

---

546.

British swimmer Lewis Gordon Pugh set a record for the longest polar swim. His extensive cold-water training gave him the power of "anticipatory thermogenesis." The mere sight of cold water sends his body temperature soaring to 101°F. How long did it take him to cover a mile in water just a few degrees above freezing?

A 20 minutes, 20 seconds
B 30 minutes, 30 seconds
C 40 minutes, 40 seconds
D 50 minutes, 50 seconds

547. Andy Roddick swings his tennis racquet with the head moving at 120 mph during the serve. Which of the following is true of the moment when his serve makes contact?

A The tennis ball is in contact with the strings for 5 milliseconds.

B The ball moves up to 8 inches laterally across the string plane of the racquet.

C The rubber ball returns approximately 30 percent of the force exerted on it.

D None of the above.

548. Approximately how far do tennis racquet strings (strung at an average of 60 pounds of tension) stretch on impact during a 120-mph serve?

A ¼ inch—or the length of a filth fly

B ½ inch—or the length of a worker carpenter ant

C 1 inch—or the length of a springtail insect

D 2 inches—or the length of many predaceous diving beetles

549. Who has the fastest serve in tennis, and how fast is it?

550. What factors add to the speed of a tennis serve?

A The speed of the racquet

B The elastic energy in the rubber of the ball

C The racquet strings

D All of the above

551. Speedo used computational fluid dynamics (CFD) computer software to create a virtual flume through which virtual swimmers were added and so flow patterns could be analyzed. What sport originally developed CFD technology?

A Skiing

B Formula One racing

C Football

D Hockey

552. During a downswing on the uneven bars, gymnasts transfer something to the fiberglass rail that is then reabsorbed in the upswing to increase rotational velocity? What is it?

A Energy

B Force

C Speed

D Mass

553. How many miles per hour does the 8,500-pound Zamboni at Madison Square Garden in New York City move?

A 9—or the distance out to sea—in miles—at which Hiromitsu Shinkawa was rescued after being swept away by the 2011 tidal wave in Japan

B 15—or the number of miles that the singer Thomas Allen, and his mule, Sal, traveled on the Erie Canal

C 22—or the flight distance in miles from the Gaithersburg, Maryland, airport to Ronald Reagan Washington National Airport in the District of Columbia

D 31—or the number of miles up to which tiger sharks and thresher sharks can zero in on targets

554. A traditional batting helmet features hard ABS plastic shell surrounding a layer of soft foam padding. It's engineered to withstand impact from a baseball traveling how fast?

A 90 mph   **B** 70 mph
C 60 mph   **D** 50 mph

555. Who has more pounds of thrust in the water: a dolphin or swimmer Michael Phelps?

556. Match the sweat rate (in quarts per hour) to the athlete.

Lightweight boxer	1.16
Baseball player	1.51
Marathoner	5.92
Triathlete	0.85
Tennis player	1.60

557. How many radio frequencies are used in a regular season football game due to wireless devices?

Ⓐ 50—or the number of copies of *Detective Comics No. 27*, the first comic book appearance of Batman, that are said to still exist.

Ⓑ 100—or the approximate number of times the Empire State Building is struck by lightning each year.

Ⓒ 200—or, in feet, the deepest point of the Mississippi River

Ⓓ 300—or the miles of patriotic bunting used in the celebration of the wedding of Prince William and Kate Middleton, now the Duke and Duchess of Cambridge

558. When an Olympic figure skater performs a triple axel, what is his or her spin rate in revolutions per minute?

Ⓐ 160 rpm—or the speed of the Ingersoll Rand air ratchet wrench

Ⓑ 220 rpm—or the maximum speed on the Artista tabletop potter's wheel

Ⓒ 420 rpm— or the speed at which some cars' engines idle

Ⓓ 620 rpm—or the lowest setting on the Grizzly G7942 Baby Drill Press

559.

The serve speeds you see on courtside digital displays are measured just as the tennis ball leaves the racquet. By the time the ball reaches the server's opponent, its speed has diminished by roughly 50 percent. What two factors cause this reduction in speed?

Ⓐ Air resistance

Ⓑ The centrifugal force of the ball

Ⓒ Backspin on the ball

Ⓓ The friction of the court surface

560. How many gallons of water does it take to make the 1-inch-thick surface of ice at Madison Square Garden?

- **A 1,000 gallons**—or the capacity of a typical septic tank holds
- **B 5,000 gallons**—or the amount of jet fuel that a Mack R-9 Refueler can hold
- **C 10,000 gallons**—or the amount of water required to fill a 21-foot aboveground swimming pool
- **D 20,000 gallons**—or the amount of beer spilled in a fourteen-car train derailment in Chilhowie, Virginia, in 2004

561. What single advance in tennis is most responsible for today's blindingly fast serves?

562. In curling, what creates friction with the stone and causes it to slowly turn as it slides down the ice curling sheet?

563. Just before the blade of a hockey player's stick hits the puck, it scrapes the ice. That friction causes the stick to bend up to 30 degrees, which preloads it like a spring. What percent of the shot's velocity does this provide?

ANSWER KEY

SCIENCE & TECHNOLOGY

1. True

2. B

3. Rocket belt. The name originated in 1953 at Bell Labs, and is still the proper name, no matter how much the technology continues to evolve.

4. Concrete: 172,000 bolts and 300,000 cubic yards of concrete were used to build the bridge.

5. A

6. D

7. C

8. Punch cards

9. Velcro

10. B

11. True

12. Thai elephant's leg: fiberglass and silicone. Japanese dolphin's tail: rubber. American eagle's beak: titanium.

13. They could repair themselves in space.

14. A

15. It mimics the human form.

16. The human. A high-school student (and self-proclaimed "weakling") from La Costa, California, beat all three robot arms in competition in March 2005.

17. Nearly five thousand, or the number of red-winged blackbirds that fell from the Arkansas sky on January 1, 2011.

18. B

19. True

20. Erno Rubik, inventor of the Rubik's Cube

21. It changes red traffic lights to green lights. MIRDs are commonly used by police, fire trucks, and ambulances.

22. Gas grill: 1960. TV remote control: 1955. Smoke detector: 1969. Sony Walkman: 1979. MRI: 1973. Superglue: 1958

23. 2000

24. A

25. Bottom pressure recorder

26. True

27. A

28. Soft contact lenses

29. B

30. A modder

31. False. Installed software can spread pieces of code among various hard-drive folders. You need to uninstall the program to free up any space.

32. Uniform resource locator

33. Hypertext markup language

34. Wireless fidelity

35. C

36. Turn it off, if it will be idle for more than two hours.

37. Multiple input, multiple output

38. True

39. Binary

40. Predict the motions of the moon and the sun

41. True, especially if you have poked holes in your ink cartridges by using refill kits, or you've unplugged your printer without turning it off first.

42. Really simple syndication

43. The world's first moving head hard disk drive

44. D

45. False

46. False. Reformatting just rearranges the information. To ensure complete destruction of data, you should either run disk-cleaning software or drill holes in the hard drive.

47. D

48. Distributed denial of service

49. C

50. Burn-in is a ghost of the static image that tattoos itself onto the screen permanently, ruining an otherwise perfectly good monitor.

51. True

52. True

53. True

54. D

55. Basic input-output system

56. 1977

57. True

58. A and D

59. Watching movies that reside on your hard drive uses less power.

60. No, although they are susceptible to image persistence, which isn't permanent.

61. Fake AV, or antivirus

62. A and C were considered as names.

63. Infrared signals

64. Brightness, contrast, color, image details, and sound

65. A

66. True

67. Using the 3G network runs down the battery faster.

68. False. Leave it in the refrigerator, not the freezer.

69. Plasma TV (210 watts): 1 watt. Cable box/digital video recorder (26 watts):

26 watts. Nintendo Wii (16 watts): 1.3 watts. DLP projector (296 watts): 3.6 watts. Desktop PC (80 watts): 4.1 watts. 20-volt battery charger (61.8 watts): 1 watt.

70. Digital light processing

71. Cathode ray tube

72. Plasma TV. The rays excite the pixels, causing them to glow in a variety of colors and shades.

73. A, C, and E

74. C

75. Neither. They tied, announcing the completion of the human genome sequence in papers published in 2001.

76. Shock muscle fibers back into a normal rhythm

77. Blocked coronary arteries

78. A

79. True. The light must be very bright, however: 405-420nm. This process leaves other useful bacteria—and your teeth and gums— unharmed.

80. A

81. A boy

82. True. Sorting through over a million reports, they found travel patterns for 10- to 2,000-mile jaunts, data that could help contain a future outbreak.

83. C

84. B

85. Inhaled air: 21 percent . Exhaled air: 15 to 16 percent. Air at sea level: 23 percent.

86. The first pacemaker is successfully implanted in a human: 1960. The first coronary bypass surgery is performed: 1967. An MRI machine is used to discern healthy tissue from cancer: 1973. The first test-tube baby is born: 1978.

87. Amino acid

88. C

89. Twenty-five thousand, or the number of polar bears worldwide

90. False. It must be extracted from white blood cells. Red blood cells lack nuclei, which is where DNA resides.

91. Fuse with a patient's living bone. It works because bone

cells attach to titanium instead of rejecting it.

92. B

93. A

94. 1987

95. Sucralose: 600 times sweeter. Aspartame: 180 times sweeter. Saccharin: 300 times sweeter. Cyclamates: 30 times sweeter.

96. True. Scientists have re-created the virus responsible for the Spanish Flu of 1918

97. A

98. E

99. D

100. A

101. Evidence of a drug overdose or poison. It can detect compounds such as heroin or arsenic that weigh less than a billionth of a gram.

102. D

103. B

104. The Monkees, in 1966

105. False. It is influenced by geological formations and the varying density of materials beneath the planet's surface.

106. Cube shaped.

That's why salt crystals clump.

107. B

108. True. A "living computer" constructed of twenty-five thousand rat neurons was linked to the flying program with an array of electrodes that passes information and instructions back and forth. By adapting to feedback pulses from the simulator, the brain has learned to control the virtual jet in a variety of weather conditions.

109. Germany and the United States

110. A highly infectious disease caused by touching or breathing in *Bacillus anthracis* spores: Anthrax. A toxin produced by the *Clostridium botulinum* bacteria: Botulism. A historical scourge caused by *Yersinia pestis* bacteria, found in rodents and their fleas: Pneumonic plague. A gas, 2-chloroethane, used during World War I: Mustard gas. A toxic, gaseous agent used in the plastic and pesticide industries: Phosgene. An odorless, colorless, tasteless gas that

attacks the nervous system: Sarin.

111. Snow crushed it. Snow in Antarctica falls but never melts.

112. D

113. No, although scientists can teleport elementary particles.

114. The "God particle." It is thought to lend mass to matter.

115. 1996

116. True. A team of Canadian scientists used nitrogen gas and an applied voltage to create it.

117. Abraham Lincoln

118. A and B

119. The Heisenberg uncertainty principle

....

NATURE

120. The Tasmanian devil. It uses its viselike jaws to kill wombats five times its weight.

121. A

122. A

123. B. By using the polarized sunlight visible at sunrise and sunset, birds can verify where north is relative to other cues,

such as the sun, the stars, and Earth's magnetic field.

124. A gecko's foot. As the lizards walks up a wall, its feet stick fast and peel off smoothly, never slipping and—since no viscous glue is involved—never losing their grip.

125. False. Many have been found since, including the Laotian rock rat, or *kha-nyou*, discovered in 2005, and the Arunachal macaque, named in 2004.

126. B

127. D

128. Later species shifted to a "rear-wheel-drive" configuration, developing stronger rear fins and legs.

129. D

130. A piranha

131. Bat: *Myotis lucifugus*. Woodchuck: *Marmota monax*. Mouse: *Peromyscus leucopus*. Eastern gray squirrel: *Sciurus carolinensis*.

132. The light generated by some animals for communication and defense.

133. B

134. Resilin, which

has the ability to recover 97 percent of its shape after deformation; high-resilience rubber can only recover about 80 percent of its shape.

135. B

136. The honeybee

137. C

138. The bullet train: The beak of the kingfisher, which dives smoothly into water. The bionic car: The boxfish, with its bony skin structure. The wind turbine: The large, irregular bumps on the leading edge of humpback whale flippers.

139. True. The laser beam creates a plasma channel that the lightning follows back to the laser source.

140. Galveston, Texas

141. A

142. A greater chance of an eruption

143. The Neva flooded in 1824; the Yangtze, in 1931.

144. A

145. More: 24 megatons for Mount St. Helens, versus 9 to10 megatons for the Mark 36

146. C

147. C

148. True

149. A

150. Avalanches

151. Over 155 mph

152. D

153. The Enhanced Fujita scale

154. True. It can also cause serious lung irritation and shortness of breath (especially for people with asthma).

155. C

156. Hot, humid, rising air often leads to thunderstorms.

157. C

158. False. Approximately 80 percent of the city was flooded.

159. B

160. Intake, Control gate, Penstock, Turbine

161. 85 percent

162. D

163. True. As the frozen water particles rise and fall they lose electrons, which collect at the bottom of a cloud, producing the negative charge that causes lightning.

163. D

164. False. You should dunk the frostbitten part of your body in warm water.

165. Just 15 minutes

166. You drink it. Waterborne illnesses won't kick in for at least three days; dehydration can kill in a single day.

167. True. Don't waste time trying to trap food. Instead, spend your energy staying warm, finding water, and signaling for rescue.

168. 80 percent

169. Asphyxiation

170. True. The metal framework will conduct lightning around you.

171. The interior part of basement, a windowless bathroom, a bedroom on the first floor, the first-floor room near a piano, to a mobile home.

172. Houston, Texas: Poor drainage with easily flooded underground tunnels. London, England: Tilts toward the southeast by 2 feet per century. Sacramento, California: Built on a flood

plain, which could be overrun by rain and meltwater from nearby mountains. St. Petersburg, Russia: Only 13 feet above sea level.

173. True

174. One gallon of clean drinking water per person, per day

175. C

176. False. You will lose more water by sweating than you will gain by building the still.

177. You can live three minutes without oxygen, three hours without warmth, three days without water, and three weeks without food.

178. One hour

TOOLS

179. C

180. Rip tooth

181. Dry powder and inert gas

182. Magnets

183. C

184. The fixed-base design

185. It is half ax and half hoe.

186. C

187. A and C

188. Beech

189. B

190. False. They *are* more efficient, but only by about 70 percent.

191. Approximately 1.5 percent carbon

192. B

193. Down—in case splintering occurs

194. It's transferred to the person operating the drill—you. It can even knock you off a ladder.

195. Yellow: straight or combination cuts. Red: Left-hand curves. Green: Right-hand curves.

196. No more than ¼ inch

197. Chisel-edge putty knife: Scraping loose paint, lifting small pieces of wallpaper, removing crumbling window putty, decal removal. Flexible 4-inch knife: Spreading drywall compound, patching cracks, light scraping. Painter's tool: Cleaning excess paint off rollers, scraping paint, and raking failed caulk out of siding and trim or weeds from sidewalk control joints. Disposable knife. Touching up putty or drywall compound on painted surfaces without leaving scuff marks.

198. False. Yes, they are designated by numbers, and yes, the larger the number, the larger the tip. But larger tips are designed to drive *heavier* screws, not lighter ones.

199. A

200. True. A recessed head requires an extra drilling step.

201. B

202. Long-nose: Cutting copper wire and bending hooks in wire to fit over terminal screws. Tongue-and-groove: Gripping pipe, plumbing fittings, and oddly shaped parts such as broken bolts. Diagonal cutters: Cutting wire in a tight spot.

203. Framing lumber, beams, and logs: Ship auger. Sheet metal, metal boxes, 1/8-inch flat and L-shaped steel or aluminum: Step drill. Standard and pressure-treated lumber: Spade bit.

Anything but masonry, glass, or tile: Twist drill.

204. A: Ordinary combustibles such as wood and paper. B: Flammable liquids such as grease, oil, and gasoline. C: An electrical fire.

205. 1 foot away from the wall per 4 feet of height

206. True

207. C

208. Grinder, disc sander, palm sander, wire brush, sandpaper

209. Drop it on the floor once or twice. The shock will scramble the magnetic domains in lightly magnetized steel.

210. False

211. D

212. Cold chisel hit with a ball-peen hammer; the cut's paw; the claw hammer; the nail puller; the hacksaw.

213. C

214. False. You want a saw with fewer teeth per inch.

215. A laser level

216. An impact driver

217. A

218. Teeth per inch

219. Orbital, random-orbit, and belt

220. C

221. P: Pull the pin. A: Aim the extinguisher at the fire's base. S: Squeeze the handle. S: Sweep the extinguisher back and forth.

222. Automatic center punch: The rapid, repeated marking of hole centers in wood and metal. Nail set: Setting nail heads. Center punch: Marking hole positions in hardened steel and cast iron. Tapered drift punch: Driving out assembly pins.

223. B

224. B

225. Synthetic rubber compounds, carbon black, granular filler on peel-off backing: Electrician's putty. Wax paper with adhesive bead: Glue strip. Fiber-reinforced plastic (7.7 to 12.6 millimeters thick) with rubber or synthetic rubber adhesive: Duct. Vinyl or PVC (7 to 8.5 millimeters thick) with adhesive that ranges from mildly to extremely sticky:

Electrical. Silicone rubber (20 to 30 millimeters thick) with peel-off backing: Self-fusing rubber. Crepe paper (4.5 to 5.5 millimeters thick) with rubber or acrylic adhesive: Masking (general). Crepe paper (5.7 to nearly 8 millimeters thick) with rubber adhesive: Masking (painting and heavy-duty).

TRANSPORTATION

226. B

227. A blown fuse.

228. False. Idling the car can do more harm than good. Instead, ask your neighbor to drive your car to work once a week while you're gone.

229. B

230. They produce power on every second piston stroke.

231. Gym socks when you turn on the heater or air-conditioner fan: Mildew growing in the moisture condensing inside your air conditioner's evaporator. Burnt carpet after you've been using the brakes a lot, or hard, or both: The brake pads are overheated. Maple syrup after the engine has warmed: Coolant is leaking. Rotten eggs when the engine is running: Hydrogen sulfide is not converting to sulfur dioxide in the catalytic converter.

232. The timing belt, chain, or gear drive

233. False. You should place the cover in the middle of the roof and unfold it toward the corners.

234. False. Most fuel-injected cars turn the fuel delivery completely off when you lift your foot from the accelerator. They still burn fuel when idling in Neutral.

235. C

236. E

237. Pneumatic struts

238. False. It takes almost no fuel to restart a warm engine.

239. D

240. D

241. If the glass gets too hot, the adhesive will set with less strength.<

242. Mineral spirits and other petroleum-based solvents kill rubber.

243. A pressure washer

244. False. When the engine isn't running, the oil pump in the transmission isn't spinning, and is therefore providing no lubrication to the gears and bearings.

245. It is poorest at near-freezing temperatures, when the pressure of the tires melts snow or ice into a thin, slick film of water.

246. C

247. A

248. True

249. Don't pump the gas. Any car with modern fuel injection should be started with your foot off the pedal.

250. A

251. Plug it into the OBD II port, a sixteen-pin connector under the dash.

252. False. It's better to sell it. Even if the odometer doesn't log any more miles, the car will lose too much value in just a year to make keeping it worthwhile.

253. D

254. Graphite. Never use penetrating oil

or anything that will amass dirt inside the mechanism.

255. True

256. 1 to 1

257. A

258. False. It changes 1 psi for every 10 degrees of outside temperature, with the pressure going down as the temp drops.

259. Back-probing

260. True

261. Connect the red to the positive terminal. The black cable goes from the negative terminal of the good battery to a ground on the car with the dead one.

262. Copper

263. True. It equalizes the water pressure, allowing you to open the door.

264. Slowly decrease speed and pull the car to the side of the road.

265. False. Tighten them in a star pattern.

266. A

267. Put the hood up.

268. True—although for short-term storage, you can simply remove the battery's negative

cable and connect a battery maintainer.

269. Ignore what's printed on the tire sidewall. It's the maximum pressure that a tire can handle, not the manufacturer's suggested setting.

270. D

271. A

272. It's hidden behind a fairly large semi-rigid piece of painted plastic.

273. True. Accident investigators use these event data recorders to determine the factors leading to a crash.

274. A and D are in both; B is found in standard automobiles only.

275. B

276. True. Grain is crushed, fermented for several days, and distilled to remove water.

277. The car, at 10 to 20 milliseconds—versus 750 milliseconds for a human

278. D

279. D

280. C

281. True

282. C

283. False. Unless your owner's manual recommends it, you're wasting money.

284. False. You will only dig the tires in deeper.

285. A

286. C

287. A

288. True

289. C

290. True

291. DC

292. Oversteering (or rear-wheel slippage)

293. RON: The RON is the research octane number. MON: The MON is the motor octane number. AKI: The AKI is the anti-knock index.

294. True

295. Hydraulic brake calipers, with only one or two moving parts. The MWA telescopes have none.

296. C

297. C

298. The Caterpillar 797B, with a 3,370 horsepower engine. The Oshkosh only powers up at 950 horsepower.

299. A

300. True

301. Wireless communication, GPS tracking, digital mapping, computing intelligence, and the Internet.

302. B

303. False

304. D

305. B

306. A

307. True

308. True

309. C

310. D

311. Near-shore, or shallow-water

312. A

313. C

314. One

315. A

316. The color increases their visibility in the event they capsize.

317. Spoilers are wing surfaces that diminish lift; they are needed during landing, when an airplane must quickly shed speed.

318. Orville Wright pilots the *Wright Flyer* in a twelve-second flight: 1903. Gabriel Voisin takes off over the Seine in a box kite glider towed by a motorboat: 1905. The first international balloon race takes place, beginning in Paris and ending in North Yorkshire, England: 1906. The first flying club, the Aeronautical Society of New York, opens: 1908. Mademoiselle Elise Deroche becomes the first qualified female pilot: 1910. The first wireless airship-to-ship message is sent: 1920.

319. D

320. B

321. To improve fuel efficiency

322. 42 percent

323. About 2 percent—approximately the same amount as U.S. dairies

324. B

325. "See and avoid."

326. B

327. Air traffic control towers, Terminal Radar Approach Control (TRACON), Air route traffic control centers

328. A

329. C

330. Magnetic levitation

331. True

332. Brown: Coastal waters. Blue: Oceans. Green: Only regional operations.

333. The USS *Ronald Reagan*

334. The canoe's top edge

335. A sailboat

336. The catch

337. C

338. A

339. It's essentially embedded in the track. The track creates a traveling magnetic field beneath the train that lifts the cars and propels them at more than 300 mph.

340. 186 mph, which is also the strongest one-minute wind gust ever recorded during a hurricane—the Great New England Hurricane of 1938

341. D

342. D

343. Unmanned aerial vehicles. There are about ten types of UAVs patrolling the skies.

344. Laptop-size

computers

345. C

346. A

347. So that infrared sensors can't spot them

348. Fly into every single hurricane

····················

HOME DIY

349. 70 percent

350. The flapper

351. The blue one

352. True. This method is called "forcing the trap."

353. Shake

354. B

355. You're checking for a leak. If any of the color shows up in the bowl, you have one.

356. False

357. A

358. Sand, gravel, water, and cement

359. A dielectric union

360. A

361. B

362. Turn on a faucet and let the water run to get rid of the smell and reestablish the water.

363. A

364. 15

365. A rigid sheet metal duct

366. Ground fault circuit interrupter

367. C

368. Fiberglass, installed between the rafters. You can blow loose-fill cellulose under the flooring and between the floor joists if you plan to continue using the attic for storage.

369. The steam from the iron makes the crushed wood fibers swell, so the dented area rises to meet the level wood around it.

370. Spray foam insulation expands to as much as 100 times its original size. And 2,400 ounces is equal to 18.75 gallons. So, yes, that's about how much foam you are now swimming in. Have fun!

371. Look at the fan blades as they rotate. If they are moving clockwise, it's set up for winter.

372. C

373. The dimmer switch, which turns off

a light 120 times per second. Bell only lived to see seventy-five.

374. C

375. About 1: slightly more than the R-value of a window of single-pane glass

376. C

377. Compound

378. Galvanization was patented by Stanislas Sorel in France in 1837. *The Scarlet Letter* hit stores in 1850.

379. Inlet water pressure, which, on average, is between 40 and 45 psi, is greater than the overpressure in an automobile tire, which averages only 32 psi.

380. C

381. True

382. C

383. Blue

384. A generator can produce more carbon monoxide than a running car. It should be kept at least 10 feet from a house.

385. A

386. Sequentially: the bottom element heats water as it enters the tank, while the top element heats water as it exits.

387. True

388. Concrete, steel, and stone

389. B

390. True

391. True

392. B

393. 3½ inches wide

394. Bendable concrete

395. D

396. True. But if you install double-glazed windows, tight doors, and insulation, you can reduce that number to 21 Btus per hour per square foot.

397. B

398. There isn't one. The nouns are synonymous.

399. 10 percent

400. C

401. Floors are supported by heavy beams called joists. These sit on sills anchored with galvanized metal straps or 1/2-inch L-bolts.

402. B

403. No. It's safer to have many individual circuits than fewer circuits with larger electrical loads.

404. Stucco

405. C

406. American sycamore, Cottonwood, Red oak, White oak

407. B. Northern white cedar will last from five to fifteen years untreated.

408. Your masterpiece will be 7,000 inches—or 583 feet, 4 inches—in height, and will indeed bypass the Washington, DC, landmark, which stands a mere 555 feet, 5 1/8 inches. Good luck with the neighborhood commission on this one.

409. B

410. Four bags of mix.

411. Standard 1/4-inch: Covers cracks. Standard 1/2-inch: Covers walls and ceilings framed on 16-inch centers. Standard 5/8-inch: Covers walls and ceilings framed on 24-inch centers. Fire-resistant 5/8-inch: Covers walls and ceilings in an attached garage or in the room above. Water-resistant 1/2-inch: Serves as a tile backer on bathroom walls. Water-

resistant 5/8-inch: Serves as a tile backer on bathroom ceilings.

412. Termites

413. B

414. Paper tape

415. Argon, an inert gas

416. "Biscuits" are thin wooden disks used for mating boards.

417. True

418. Hot-dipped galvanized, or corrosion-resistant

419. That the foundation is shifting

420. A

421. D

422. Driving in nails at an angle

423. The bottom

424. Hot wire: Ungrounded conductor. Neutral wire: Grounded conductor. Grounding wire: Equipment-grounding conductor.

425. A

426. The former

427. Jack. He knows that leaving them just shy of the surface allows the siding to expand and contract.

428. C

429. True

430. True

431. False. Triple glazing is about five times as efficient as single glazing.

432. Balloon framing. This method, which utilizes long studs to frame the building, is rarely used anymore.

433. Spackling paste: Filling small cracks and minor dents in wood, masonry, and metal. Colored wood putty: Concealing nail holes and minor surface blemishes. An epoxy stick: Odd jobs, repairing metal, or resetting hardware on knockdown furniture. Epoxy-based wood filler: Rebuilding painted wood architectural elements, such as windowsills.

434. A control joint

435. Vertical grain. It expands and contracts less across its width, and this stability improves paint longevity.

436. False. You should wash from the bottom to the top to minimize streaking, then rinse from the top to the bottom.

437. B

438. B

439. B

440. A vacuum-breaker fitting

441. C

442. B

443. It expands as it cures.

444. The first cut you should make when felling a tree is on the side where the tree is going to fall.

445. C

446. Gable: A roof whose edges extend over the wall, as in classic Cape Cod houses. Gambrel: A symmetrical roof found in Dutch Colonial houses, with two slopes on each side. Mansard: A Victorian-style four-sided roof with two slopes on each side, the upper less steep than the lower. Saltbox: An asymmetric roof with one side topping a second story and the other sloping down to top the first floor on the other side.

447. B

448. About three thousand

449. 1981

450. B

451. Unseen galaxies

452. 39 percent

453. C

454. A, because it takes thousands, millions or, in some cases, billions of years for light from faraway stars to reach us.

455. The heliosheath

456. The National Aeronautics and Space Administration (NASA): 1958. The Russian Aviation and Space Agency/The Russian Federal Space Agency: 1992. The European Space Agency (ESA): 1973. The Canadian Space Agency (CSA): 1989. The Japan Aerospace Exploration Agency (JAXA): 2003. The China National Space Administration (CNSA): 1993.

457. C

458. B

459. 2,400 feet, or less than half a mile

460. A

461. *Spirit, Sojourner,* and *Opportunity,* launched by the U.S.; *Mars 2 Prop-M* and *Mars 3 Prop-M,* launched by the U.S.S.R.)

462. Six

463. Up to four years

464. Approximately 63,360 feet or 12 miles

465. American Dennis Tito, who travelled on the Russian *Soyuz TM-32* in 2001

466. C

467. A

468. D

469. A. The turtles survived, though they lost 10 percent of their body weight.

470. Nine

471. *Endeavour* was the final shuttle made. (*Atlantis* was the final shuttle flown.)

472. Thermal protection system

473. True. Footage released in 2007 showed a test flight from a remote site in western Texas, where an approximately 30-foot-high un-manned craft owned by Bezos took off vertically and rose 285 feet before landing—intact—on a concrete pad. In September 2011, some reports

474. A

475. Seven years. It used a gravity assist from Venus (twice), Earth, and Jupiter to build momentum for the trip.

476. Ham

477. *Explorer 1*

478. Slowing a craft by flying it through a planet's upper atmosphere

479. B, by Russian Valeri Polyakov.

480. A

481. His boots

482. 23 inches

483. C

484. *Pioneer 10* left the solar system in 1983.

485. D

486. At 50 miles above the Earth's surface

487. Only 24

488. Pluto

489. Telstar

490. *Phoenix*

491. True

492. C

493. B

494. About sixty are known to have single moonlets formed by debris from colliding asteroids.

495. Saturn

496. Saturn

497. C

498. Dark matter

499. C

500. D

501. Mercury and Venus

502. False. These are comets.

503. Saturn: Titan. Jupiter: Ganymede. Mars: Phobos. Neptune: Triton.

504. There is one common thread to life on Earth that scientists know for certain: all life here is composed of the same basic building blocks. All proteins are made of compounds known as amino acids. All genes are made of molecules known as nucleotides, which are attached to a backbone made of phosphate and a sugar called ribose.

505. B

506. True. Astronomers have discovered more than 1,200 likely planets.

507. Super glue

508. D, located in Arizona.

509. More. It would actually take about 272 billion of them.

SPORTS

510. The snowmobile

511. Ethanol

512. Twenty. Some races can even chew up fifteen sets of tires.

513. The All-American Soap Box Derby, the third-oldest "car" race in the United States after the Indy 500 and the Pikes Peak International Hill Climb

514. Lactic acid

515. 50 to 60 percent

516. C

517. False. He has a headphone built into in his helmet so he can listen to his coach, but he has no mic.

518. Five races, maximum

519. B

520. A minimum of three bike lengths. It is just enough distance to keep riders from drafting one another.

521. D

522. A prolonged wreck

523. 12 inches

524. C

525. Volleyball: 112 mph. Shot put: 30 mph. Tennis ball: 155 mph. Ping pong ball: 70 mph. Water polo ball: about 65 mph. Soccer ball : about 82 mph.

526. C

527. Longer skis

528. B

529. Frozen grass

530. The Defense Advanced Research Projects Agency is a contest for driverless vehicles.

531. C

532. C

533. B

534. A curveball. A 94-mph fastball leaves the bat 3 mph faster than a 78-mph curveball—but it travels 442 feet, compared with the curveball's 455 feet.

535. About 70 percent

536. C

537. Microfiber

538. A gyroball is a pitch that breaks horizontally (without sinking) as it nears the batter, as though shrugging off gravity.

539. B

540. False. The extreme football impact rates a 150.

541. B

542. Concrete. More recent "soft walls" have been made from Cellofoam, layered PVC, and other more forgiving materials.

543. A

544. True

545. A

546. B

547. A

548. C

549. Andy Roddick, who maxed out at 155 mph

550. D

551. B

552. A

553. A

554. B

555. A dolphin's tail flip generates about 200 pounds of thrust—triple Michael Phelps's best effort.

556. Lightweight boxer: 0.85. Baseball player: 1.16. Marathoner: 1.51.

Triathlete:1.60. Tennis player: 5.92.

557. D

558. C

559. D

560. C

561. The oversize racquet heads

562. Tiny drops of frozen water, or "pebbles," on the ice

563. 50 percent

PHOTOGRAPHY CREDITS

Getty Images: 148, 157; SSPL/ Science Museum: 20; HF Davis: 89; Ryan McVay: 107; NASA/Science Faction: 143; Simon Bruty/Sports Illustrated: 158
iStockphoto: 13, 64, 86, 109, 164; Frank Leung: 3, 9; Luminis: 4 top, 95; Paul Johnson: 4 bottom, 155; Andrew Rich: 7; Alperium: 10; Pagadesign: 15; Baris Simsek: 16; Rafal Dubiel: 18; Rouzes: 22; Tom England: 25; Ingram Publishing: 27; Jaroslaw Wojcik: 28; Antti-Pekka Lehtinen: 31; Leah-Anne Thompson: 32; Volodymyr Goinyk: 35; Ralf Hettler: 37; Craig Dingle: 39; Jami Garrison: 40; Sascha Burkard: 42; Jill Chen: 44; Rainer Albiez: 47; Victor Zastol Skiy: 49; Shannon Stent: 51; Marco Maccarini: 53; Hector Mandel: 55; Tom Schmucker: 57; Tomas Vrtal: 58; Konstantin Kirillov: 60; Mikhail Basov: 63; Christian Carroll: 67; Feng Yu: 68; Robert Faric: 71; Joan Vicent Cantó Roig: 72; John Panella: 75; Deborah Maxemow: 77; Martti Salmela: 78; Hart Photography: 80; James Steidl: 83; Amelia Johnson: 84; Peter Mah: 90; Marc Sublet: 93; Tony Tremblay: 96; Brigitte Smith: 98; Jared DeCinque: 101; Luigi De Zotti: 103; Tatiana Popova: 105; Skip O'Donnell: 110; Julia Nichols: 113; Milan Vasicek: 115; Joy Fera: 116; Dmitry Kutlayev: 118; Steve Gray: 121; Sergiy Tryapitsyn: 122; Matthew Valentine: 124; Leslie Banks: 126; Carla Lisinski: 128; James Benet: 131; Teresa Hurst: 133; Chad Purser: 134; George Toubalis: 137; Aaron Rutten: 145; Stephan Hoerold: 146; Sumners Graphics Inc: 151; Maxim Tupikov: 152; Gevorg Gevorgyan: 161; Todd Taulman: 163
NASA: Jet Propulsion Laboratory: 141 AFP: 139